Functional Weight Gain
for Athletes

Functional Weight Gain for Athletes

Sean Ross, CSCS, OTR/L

Copyright 2019 by Sean Ross

All rights reserved. Except for brief passages used in book reviews, no part of this book may be reproduced in any form without the express written permission of the author. For requests to use material from the book or to order additional copies, you may contact him here:

    Sean Ross, CSCS, OTR/L
    Box 7808
    Little Rock, AR 72217
    Rossstrengthandspeed@gmail.com
    RossStrengthandSpeed.com

ISBN: 978-1-7337964-1-5

Book and cover design: H. K. Stewart

Printed in the United States of America

This book is printed on archival-quality paper that meets requirements of the American National Standard for Information Sciences, Permanence of Paper, Printed Library Materials, ANSI Z39.48-1984.

To Mom and Pop

Contents

Acknowledgements 9

Chapter 1: The Benefits of and Obstacles to
　　Gaining Functional Weight 11

Chapter 2: Basic Nutrition 19

Chapter 3: General Eating Principles 23

Case Study: Adam. 27

Chapter 4: Eating to Gain Healthy Weight 29

Chapter 5: Practical Tips That Can Change Your Life! 35

Case Study: Monroe 41

Chapter 6: Pre- and Post-Workout Nutrition 43

Chapter 7: Supplementation 49

Chapter 8: Poor Man's Eating 61

Case Study: Roli 69

Chapter 9: Eating on the Go 71

Chapter 10: Strength and Speed Development 79

Case Study: Thomas 88

Chapter 11: The Weight Room 89

Chapter 12: Three- and Four-Day Examples 95

Chapter 13: Effort 109

Chapter 14: Monitoring Strength Progress 113

Case Study: Ty *116*

Chapter 15: In-Season Weight Retention 119

Chapter 16: Steroids 123

Chapter 17: The Best We Can Be 127

About the Author 129

Acknowledgements

Special thanks go out to my excellent English teachers at Christian Brothers High School, who taught me to the best of their ability but would never guess that I would ever write a book; to the many clients over the years who trusted me in their training and volunteered to be my laboratory rats; to my longest tenured training client and author/editor Jay Jennings, who encouraged me to write this book and was instrumental in making it come to print; to Mike Boyle, who spent fifteen minutes on the phone with me in 2003 as I was learning to train athletes and pointed me on a path that would change my life; to my brother Marty, who encouraged me as a twelve-year-old to lift weights by paying me a quarter a week; and to those who made fun of me as a teen for being skinny and lit a fire under me to do something about it.

Chapter 1:
The Benefits of and Obstacles to Gaining Functional Weight

Who Needs to Gain Weight?

There are many books and videos produced to help one lose weight and get leaner. After all, America is the fifth fattest country in the world and billions of dollars have been spent on diets, training, and supplements to combat this epidemic. Few books, however, have been written to help someone gain weight, or as some call them, "those lucky SOBs!" This book will give practical solutions to those that desire to add healthy weight to their bodies. It is based on acquired scientific knowledge years of training hundreds of athletes in my own gym where a laboratory environment can be utilized, and from once being a hard gainer myself and knowing what a struggle it can be to gain the next pound.

"Why would anyone want to gain weight?" is a question most often asked by overweight people that would love to trade places with a hard gainer. Athletes may need to gain weight (build muscle) in order to increase their strength and power. Additional strength and power can translate into being faster, hitting a ball farther, jumping higher, etc. It is important to realize that the goal is to improve overall horsepower. Gaining fat or even muscle that has been acquired by non-functional training methods can often make someone slower or less powerful. Think of it like adding five hundred pounds to the body of a car but doing nothing to the engine. Another example would be to add a ten-pound vest to someone and have them run a forty-meter sprint, then run one without the vest. Of course the vested sprinter would run much slower. However, if the additional ten pounds is primarily muscle that has been acquired through good functional training, then there is a good chance the sprint times will improve. Even if one were to gain ten pounds while sprint times and vertical jump stayed the same, he/she would be able to produce much greater horsepower.

Many times additional mass is needed for contact sports such as football to protect the body and give it more armor. Linemen may need to be heavier to gain a leverage advantage over an opponent that is big and powerful. While many athletes in sports such as soccer, swimming, and cycling may not want to be heavier, they most certainly could use more strength and power. Most could use a few more pounds of functional muscle, and many could improve their performance by following more of a gainer's diet if they are chronically underfed to begin with.

Another benefit from gaining weight is to improve an athlete's body profile for recruiting purposes. I have seen many talented high school athletes be overlooked by college recruiters because they were twenty pounds underweight for their positions. This is unfair sometimes, as a good college strength and nutrition program should be able to physically develop them in a progressive manner. Many colleges expect the high school recruit to be "game size" or have a grown man's body before they even attend the first college practice. This often rewards those with superior genetics or who have physically matured much earlier than others. Sometimes these "early bloomers" reach their genetic potential or "top out" early and fail to develop much more once they reach college. Sometimes they have always been the biggest and strongest of their youth peers and lack the work ethic that a hard gainer has and get "out developed" once the hard gainer gets in an optimum training environment. A good example is Clay Matthews Jr., now with the Green Bay Packers. Clay was a 190-pound walk-on at the University of Southern California when he arrived on campus. His combination of relentless pursuit of improvement combined with the guidance of USC strength coach Chris Carlisle turned him into a 240-pound All-American and now multiple-time NFL Pro Bowl selection. By the way, Coach Carlisle won two National Championships at USC and followed USC head coach Pete Carroll to the NFL's Seattle Seahawks, where they won the Super Bowl in his fourth year and was one play away from winning another. The Seahawks also have the lightest, but most athletic, offense line in the NFL…functional muscle at its best.

    Finally, some people want to gain weight just for appearances. They feel skinny, which can affect their self-confidence and social life. Let's face it, many girls dig a "hunk" instead of a "beanpole" and many guys dig girls that aren't built like a skeleton. Whether your goal is to improve in athletics or to look better at the pool, adding functional muscle to an underweight frame is possible with a proper game plan.

Obstacles to Gaining Weight

Of course not everyone can gain muscle at the same rate. After all, if it were that easy then everyone who has ever lifted weights or had a protein drink would be walking around looking like an Olympic sprinter. There are many factors that may interfere with gaining muscle before looking at calorie consumption as the simple answer. Genetics play a major role. A mesomorph (naturally muscular physique) is going to respond to training much faster than an ectomorph (naturally thin), while an endomorph (naturally fat) may gain body fat at a much faster rate than desirable. It is important to note that most people are a blend of the body types, such as an ecto-meso or a meso-endo. Some ectomorphs use genetics as an excuse and do not show the dedication in the weight room or with the knife and fork to overcome a fixable problem. Of course they may never become "a monster" but twenty pounds of muscle on a skinny frame can do wonders both physically and psychologically.

Another factor that often limits progress is a lack of money. Sufficient money is needed for gym fees, supplements, and food. Extended work hours to try to make ends meet cuts down on the available hours to train also. Busy school schedules or travel schedules with work can also affect consistent training and eating plans. Inconsistency and lack of planning are some of the biggest obstacles that can be corrected by behavioral modifications and discipline. Taking Adderall, which many students do to combat attention deficit disorder, can greatly diminish appetite. It's amazing how many with ADD have no problem memorizing every word to a rap song but somehow struggle to concentrate on algebra while watching TV or texting friends. The easy solution is to give them the one performance enhancing drug that *is* acceptable to parents, Adderall. Good luck trying to gain weight while on Adderall, 'cause it ain't happening!

Excess alcohol consumption can be another limiting factor. Alcohol has no nutritional value and primarily consists of empty calories void of protein, carbs, or fats. It can dehydrate you and suppress your appetite—not good if you're a hard gainer who has to stay on a strict schedule of eating and training in order to gain weight. Studies have also shown that excess alcohol can lower testosterone levels, a vital hormone in the muscle-building process. Of course many gain weight from regular drinking, and if a beer belly doesn't bother you as part of your weight gain then by all means keep on drinking! Many times the same people that complain about not having enough money to buy food or supplements always find a way to buy alcohol. I'm not saying that you should totally eliminate alcohol consumption (unless you are under legal drinking age of course), but you should limit its consumption if muscle gain is a priority. A good rule of thumb might be to limit yourself to two drinks a week while gaining weight is a priority. Go eat a meal or drink a weight-gainer shake instead. It will do you much more good than a six pack of beer.

Lack of knowledge is also a barrier to gaining weight. Many do not know how to train or eat in order to maximize their gains. Many do not take the time to learn from others or educate themselves, and instead keep doing the same strategy with no positive result. While the internet provides a limitless supply of information on training and nutrition, which route to take is often confusing too. Hopefully your reading this book will help weed out many of the side routes and lead you down a road to a good system that will help you gain horsepower-producing muscle.

An often overlooked aspect with obtaining weight-gaining goals, or any other goals for that matter, is a lack of good social support. The people you hang out with need to be supportive of your desire to gain weight. Better yet, if your friends also have similar goals, it makes it a lot easier to pursue them. For instance, if you are going out with similarly driven friends on a Saturday night, then they will have a similar mindset as you and you won't feel embarrassed about your behaviors. You all will probably include a nutritious meal before you go out, consume very limited if any alcohol, keep appropriate snacks or a protein shake in the car for easy access, and dine on a nutritious meal before going home at a reasonable hour to get a good muscle-building, regenerative sleep. Compare that to going out with pot-smoking, beer-guzzling friends that don't care if they look like a marshmallow man with sticks for arms and a soft round body.

Many of your friends who also train may be complacent and not care if they make any gains year after year. They will continue to do the same habits and have no ambition when it comes to setting and obtaining fitness goals. Many girls who want to add weight by gaining muscle will be laughed at by other girls who think being skinny is the ideal. Your boyfriends or girlfriends may make fun of you for having such goals and modifying your lifestyle. If at all possible, dump them and find someone who is supportive. Life is hard enough to succeed at without having the ones that supposedly love us try to hold us down from becoming the best version of ourselves possible. Chances are, if they are not supportive in your fitness goals, they won't be with your ambitions with education or work either. Instead of looking to you as an inspiration and motivating them to become a better version of themselves, these human anchors would rather pull you down to their level so they won't feel bad about their own lack of ambition. "Misery loves company" applies in several areas of life.

Chapter 2:
Basic Nutrition

Nutrition is an often overlooked factor in gaining good functional muscle. You can be following the most sophisticated weight-training program there is but without sufficient food intake there will be marginal gains at best. The fat-loss guru Alwyn Cosgrove says diet is No. 1, and diet is No. 2, then training is No. 3 when it comes to losing body fat. I think the same could be true with gaining weight. When you lift weights, you are actually tearing down muscle. Nutrition and recovery are what build the muscles back larger. If you aren't getting enough of the right nutrients in, you will be in a constant state of overtraining and muscles will not grow.

Before getting more specific about nutrition, I would like to give credit to Dr. John Berardi of Precision Nutrition. In a world of millions of nutritional opinions and plans, Dr. Berardi's Precision Nutrition program helped me to understand and simplify a system that is a great blend of performance, body composition, and health. Many of my suggestions in this book are based on what I've learned from him, as well as my thirty-five years of practical applications from my own experiences. I highly recommend taking his Precision Nutrition Certification program if you want to greatly improve your nutritional knowledge.

The macronutrients that you need to have a basic understanding of are protein, carbohydrates, and fats. Protein is composed of amino acids, which are the building blocks of muscle. A good supply of protein in both quantity and quality is necessary to rebuild muscle after a workout to become stronger and bigger. Think of building a house. The house is going to be more structurally sound if it is built with cement and brick than it would be if it were built with straw and mud. The quality of protein from sources such as eggs, lean beef, bison, venison, poultry, fish, dairy, and protein powders will be much more anabolic than inferior sources such as soy, which has been linked to increased estrogen levels in high amounts, or peanut better, which is much more of a fat source than a protein. A PBJ (or with honey) is fine if you are trying to increase your overall calories, but it should be consumed with a quality protein source such as skim milk with a scoop of protein powder added. Read the labels of what you are eating. You may be surprised to find that what you thought was a protein may not be. Plant-based proteins should be carefully blended with other protein sources to insure that all of the essential amino-acid requirements (those that can't be made by the body and must be supplied by the diet) are met.

In addition to the structural benefits, protein plays a vital role in hormone and enzyme function, as well as strengthening the immune system. If protein degradation is greater than protein intake, enzymes and structural proteins that form cells are cannibalized. If this occurs for an extended time, vital functions shut down.

Carbohydrates are typically looked at as energy producers. The three major classes of carbohydrates are monosaccharides, oligosaccharides, and polysaccharaides. These are broken down and released into the bloodstream as glucose. Glucose is used as energy, and if blood glucose is high while the muscle and liver storage supplies are full, excess glucose can be transformed into body fat. For simplification purposes in this book, we will often refer to starchy carbs (potatoes, rice, oatmeal, breads, pastas, etc.) and fibrous carbs (spinach, tomatoes, broccoli, celery, squash, etc.). Simple carbs (sugar, fruits, sports drinks) quickly raise blood sugar but don't provide sustained energy like the complex carbs typically found in the starchy carb category. All of these forms of carbs have a function in optimizing weight and performance management as well as overall health.

Fats traditionally have been frowned upon by those uneducated about their function. Government recommendations in the '70s and '80s suggested diets be virtually void of dietary fat, and as a result obesity rates rose tremendously. Dietary fat functions as an energy source, helps manufacture and balance hormones, forms cell membranes, forms our brain and nervous systems, helps transport fat soluble vitamins, and provides essential fatty acids that the body can't make.

Fats are divided into three categories: saturated, monounsaturated, and polyunsaturated. Saturated fats are typically found in foods such as tropical oils, eggs, and red meat. Monounsaturated fats include olive oil, avocados, and nuts. Polyunsaturated fats include the Omega 3s (flax, salmon, walnuts, etc.) and the Omega 6 (canola, safflower, etc.). Another fat group is the trans fats, which are produced primarily from industrial fat processing to make oils taste better and last longer, hence good for the company's profit margin. Trans fats raise bad cholesterol and contribute to heart disease. Trans fats also lower the good cholesterol. When consuming a diet consisting of natural, unprocessed foods, accumulating high amounts of harmful trans fats is nearly impossible.

Good general guidelines for fat consumption are to have a balance between saturated, monounsaturated, and polyunsaturated fats. Omega 3 ratios should greatly exceed Omega 6 ratios for the anti-inflammation properties that Omega 3s possess. Also, carb intake should be inversely proportional with dietary fat intake. If the diet is high in carbs, which will be typically recommended in this book for those hard gainers wishing to add mass, the fat intake should be lower. After sufficient mass is gained and some body fat is desired to be lost, then a higher fat/lower carb intake can be utilized. These general guidelines for the classification and functions of protein, fats, and carbohydrates in the previous paragraphs are meant for those that have virtually no knowledge of general nutrition, which many I have found do not. It is in no way intended to provide great detail. In a world of a million different dietary resources and "what should I believe?" questions, I again recommend the writings and Precision Nutrition Course of John Berardi for those wanting to learn more about general nutrition. That being said, let's dive into learning how to eat in order to pack on some functional muscle.

Chapter 3:
General Eating Principles

Regardless of whether you are trying to gain or lose weight, protein should be consumed with every meal. As stated before, protein is necessary to build muscle broken down from previous workouts and to preserve existing muscle from being used as fuel in future workouts. General guidelines for the amount of protein eaten each meal are a palm-sized portion for females and two palm-sized portions for males. More specific recommendations are at least 1.0 to 1.5 grams per pound of body weight over the course of a day. A number of twenty to forty grams per meal for women and forty to sixty grams per meal for men may put you in this range if you are eating five to six meals a day. If you are only eating two to three meals a day, the portion sizes should be much larger. One reason to eat every two to three hours is that it is easier to reach high daily nutrient totals. If you are only able to eat two to four times a day then the meals should be much larger to reach high daily totals. We often hear how it is important to eat smaller more frequent meals but it is possible to still gain muscle by eating larger, less frequent meals if at the end of the day your nutrient goals are reached. It may be difficult to consume such large servings for many people, and supplementation may be necessary. (We will discuss practical strategies for this solution later.)

I also believe nontraining people should still follow the protein-with-every-meal rule for their general health and weight control. Many elderly people at a cafeteria go for the "vegetable plate" and choose no meat portion. Most do this thinking they are eating more healthy when in fact it may be one of the biggest factors in aging since our cells are constantly being regenerated and high-quality amino acids from protein will be the building blocks for the new cells. A higher protein diet will also help strengthen their immune system and balance the protein/carb/fat ratio better for insulin sensitivity and ultimately control of excess body-fat accumulation.

Fibrous carbohydrates (green beans, broccoli, squash, spinach, tomatoes, etc.) should also be consumed with every meal. At least a handful or two portion sizes will be sufficient. Even protein drinks can easily be made healthier by adding a handful of spinach or a greens powder supplement. Fibrous carbs help control insulin levels and provide fiber to slow down food absorption and allow a steady release of nutrients to the bloodstream. The exception to this is a pre- or post-workout protein/carb drink where fast absorption is desired. Eating lots of fibrous vegetables is also great for overall health with their numerous antioxidant powers. Don't be like some people and say, "Eww, I just can't stand eating vegetables!" You're not five years old. Eat first for function, not taste.

Starchy carbs (potatoes, rice, oatmeal, whole-grain pastas and breads, beans, etc.) should be eaten with every meal if you are trying to gain weight. Those wanting to lose weight should save the majority of their starchy carb consumption for post-workout meals. The amount of starchy carbs consumed each meal will depend on your daily goals, but it is still a good idea to get the largest portions in the post workout meal when the metabolism is at its highest. For the ectomorph, carbohydrates should make up to fifty percent of the diet's total calories.

Simple carbohydrates (those from fruit, sugary drinks and foods, etc.) do play a role in gaining weight. A three-to-one ratio of fibrous carbs to fruit, which contains the simple carbohydrate fructose, is generally recommended for those on a gaining diet. Fruit juices should be avoided or at least saved for post workout since they contain large amounts of concentrate sugar without the fiber of the whole fruit itself. Ice cream, chocolate milk, etc. can play a role in increasing calorie totals, which we will discuss later. I tell my athletes to limit soft drinks to two per week at most, even diet sodas. Soft drinks are for watching a movie at the cinema with a bucket of popcorn, not for drinking with meals. Get into the habit of drinking water (at least two to three liters per day) or unsugared green tea (has good antioxidants). Another recommendation is .5–1.0 ounce of water per pound of bodyweight per day. Your skin will thank you and your dentist too if you cut out the regular soda consumption. Refer back to the "eat for function, not for taste" section a few paragraphs ago if you are one who bitches about drinking water instead of Mountain Dew with meals. Another water tip is to, of course, consume more in hot, humid environment. Also, add a half a teaspoon of salt to your liter of water or sports drink to make it a better electrolyte mix in hot conditions.

Healthy fats should be added to the daily diet. Generally, fat consumption is inversely proportional starchy carbohydrate consumption. Since the goal of most of you reading this book is to gain weight, a higher starchy carbohydrate/lower fat diet should be followed. The total calories from fat should be around twenty to thirty percent. Remember that a gram of fat has nine calories whereas a gram of carbohydrate has four calories per gram, so the twenty to thirty percent amount is of calories not total grams. We will cover specific calorie requirements later in the book. Fat consumption, regardless of the total grams, should be divided roughly into one third from saturated fats, one third from monounsaturated fats, and one third from polyunsaturated fats. To simplify this, don't worry about adding saturated fats. You will get enough from lean meats. Be sure to add some almonds, mixed nuts, olive oil, or avocado/guacamole for your monounsaturates, and for polyunsaturates take fish oil capsules rich in EPA and DHA since they have more good anti-inflammatory active Omega-3. The total Omega-3 consisting of EPA and DHA should fall between one and three grams per day. For example, if your one-gram capsules contain 350 grams of EPA/DHA (read the label to find out), then you should take three to eight capsules per day.

Case Study: Adam

Adam started training with me in December following his junior year of football for Little Rock's Pulaski Academy, best know as "the team that never punts." He was 6' 4", 185 pounds and ran an official 4.72 forty-yard dash. He had always had trouble gaining weight. After analyzing his diet, I realized he was not consuming enough starchy carbohydrates to fuel his high exercise demands and fast metabolism. I told Adam to start eating three to four slices of whole-grain bread with his meals. Since each slice had about 100 calories, twenty grams of carbs, and a bonus five grams of protein, he was adding a significant amount of nutrients to his daily, weekly, and monthly total. He started carrying loaves of bread to school every day and became known as "the bread man." He gained a pound or two a week and started the next season in August weighing 230 pounds. He gained forty-five pounds in eight months by simply eating more bread with his meals and snacks! In addition, by following a well-designed speed, mobility, plyometric, strength, and power program while he was gaining, he was again clocked at 4.72 in the forty while his vertical jump improved to thirty-three inches. If your speed or vertical jump stay the same while you are gaining, you are actually producing much more horsepower than what you did at a lighter weight. Adam also lead the state in sacks while being named All-State his senior season.

Chapter 4:
Eating to Gain Healthy Weight

Most people who want to gain weight are ectomorphs or young mesomorphs. Ectomorphs are naturally on the skinny side with long, thin limbs and very fast metabolisms. They are usually the ones who say "I just can't gain weight no matter what I do." They have a low body fat percentage, at least until they discover habitual beer drinking. Mesomorphs are the lucky ones who genetically have broad shoulders, small waists, and can put on muscle at a much faster rate than ectomorphs. Many young mesomorphs may be on the thin side, but realize they respond well to weight training. This encourages them to strive to gain more muscle fast. Endomorphs struggle with keeping their body fat levels down and typically will be reading books on losing weight than gaining.

Generally speaking, if you are lean to begin with, you may gain about seventy percent muscle and thirty percent fat while on a gaining program. If you are fat to begin with, you may gain about thirty percent muscle and seventy percent fat. Obviously, if you are fat to begin with, it's probably not the best idea to be trying to gain weight unless you are trying out for your school sumo wrestling team. If you are an ectomorph (thin) and trying to gain weight, don't worry about gaining a little fat along the way. Those who want to gain muscle without any fat typically undereat and make no gains at all or gain weight at a very slow pace. When you reach your desired weight or you feel like getting leaner for the beach or your sport, it will be easy to modify your diet and training and drop the excess fat. Be cautious though at the traditional "bulking up" phases that give you an excuse to eat total crap and gain more fat than muscle. It is easy to see big increases on the scale and think you are "getting huge" when in reality your gut is the only thing that is getting huge. Periodic before and after pictures can be a reality check to keep from getting out of hand. How fast and how much muscle one can gain in a given time is hard to determine. Some say it is impossible to gain more than a pound or two a month. I've had clients gain twenty+ pounds in three months and most of it be muscle. I think many skinny people have been underfed for years, and once they start eating and training correctly, their initial gains come at an alarming rate. These gains may eventually slow to that of a typical ectomorph, but the initial rate of gains may defy the experts' scientific theories. Each person is different. Each has different rates of genetic potential and each has different behavior characteristics in how hard they train, how consistent they follow the nutrition plan, etc. While we can't control our genetics, we can control our behaviors. With behavior habits being consistently followed over years, I feel it is possible to even change our DNA, so to speak, and turn ourselves into more of a mesomorph instead of an ectomorph.

Getting Precise with the Plan

Many times gaining weight can be solved by simply eating more food until a positive energy balance is reached. Take in more food in than you burn off, and presto, muscle starts coming on. With ectomorphs (remember, naturally thin) this sometimes means consuming as much as eighteen to twenty-two times their body weight in calories. An example would be that a 150-pound ectomorph may have to consume 2700–3300 calories to initiate gaining weight. Some may need fewer calories if they were eating much less to begin with. An additional 500 calories to them may be all they need. Since different people will gain at different rates, as long as you are gaining at least a pound every week or two, then keep consuming the same amount. Remember, a pound a week may not sound like much, but fifteen more pounds added to a 150-pound frame is a whopping ten percent increase in body mass in only fifteen weeks! Think about an eighteen-year-old 150-pounder needing 936 weeks of his life (eighteen x fifty-two weeks/year) to get to 150 pounds suddenly increasing his/her body weight by ten percent in only fifteen weeks! Keep this pace up for a year and you're looking at a 200 pounder. Of course this rate of gain won't last forever, but I often use these examples to those that are discouraged by gaining "only" a pound a week. Remember also to adjust the calories and recalculate as you gain. Eighteen times (of calories) your body weight for a 170 pounder is more than eighteen times for a 150-pounder. Calorie demands are higher for those who have more muscle, and more should be consumed to reach a positive energy balance.

Increasing your calories to eighteen to twenty times your body weight does not give you a free pass to dismiss any sound nutritional guidelines. Ectomorphs (the skinny type) should strive for a diet consisting of fifty percent carbs, with the majority of these being from complex carbs (rice, potatoes, oatmeal, whole-grain pasta, etc.) as opposed to simple carbs (sugars and fruits). This does not mean that simple carbs should be eliminated, but more complex choices should be made first, then simple carbs to add more calories if needed. A good general rule for fruit consumption should be a three-to-one ratio of fibrous carbs (green veggies, etc.) to fruit for those trying to gain and a five-to-one veggie-to-fruit ratio for those trying to get leaner. Complex carbs should be consumed at every meal for endomorphs desiring to gain.

Protein, which should be consumed every meal regardless of wanting to gain or lose, should be about thirty-five percent of your diet. Again, aim for 1.0–1.5 grams per pound of body weight. An easy way to reach this 1.5 goal is to simply shoot for one gram per pound of body weight from sources such as chicken, fish, eggs, beef, powder, etc., and the remaining protein comes from the smaller amounts found in vegetables and nuts, etc. In other words, count the grams from the optimum sources and don't worry about counting the grams from other sources. Those can be considered bonus grams. Make protein sources fairly lean so that total fat consumption is about fifteen percent of the total calories for the day. Fat has traditionally taken a bad rap for those wanting to get leaner by following a "low fat" diet, but, actually, most wanting to lose weight benefit from a higher fat (forty percent) and lower carb (twenty-five percent) diet. Remember when calculating fat calories that a gram of fat has nine calories where a gram of protein or carbs has four calories.

An example for a 150-pound ectomorph trying to calculate daily requirements to gain would be as follows:

body weight 150 x 18–20 = 2700–3000 calories
50% carbs • 30% protein • 20% fat

2700–3000 calories ÷ 50% = 1350–1500 calories carbs
▼
÷ 4 (4 calories/gram carbs) = 338–375 grams carbs

2700–3000 calories ÷ 30% = 810–900 calories protein
▼
÷ 4 (4 calories/grams protein) = 203–225 grams protein

2700–3000 calories ÷ 20% = 540–600 calories fat
▼
÷ 9 (9 calories/grams fat) = 60–67 grams fat

If you are eating five times a day, then each meal should roughly be sixty-eight to seventy-five grams of carbs, forty to forty-five grams of protein, and twelve to fourteen grams of fat. Less feeding a day would require more of each per meal and more feedings may be smaller to reach the daily totals.

Of course if you have been grossly underfed prior to starting a weight gaining diet, it may not be necessary to get eighteen to twenty times body weight in calories. Someone eating 1500 calories a day may only need to increase to 2000+ to start gaining. It is a great idea to make a three-day eating log before you start trying to gain. Calculate the calories and macronutrient totals. Many will be shocked to find how few calories, particularly protein calories, they have been consuming when they thought they were eating a lot. Not many will take the time to keep up with daily consumption totals. Phone apps do make it easier to record for those that want to. It is not always necessary to keep up with totals if you follow the general eating guidelines recommended earlier and simply eat more per meal than what you were before. Finding the right balance that works for you is key, but following the same plan that hasn't been working while hoping that it will magically start working is wasting time. If you don't want to take the time to record your daily calorie totals, I would recommend that you at least record the number of protein grams for a few days to insure that they are being met. If you are not a pure ectomorph and are still trying to gain weight, it may not be necessary to consume up to fifty percent of your calories form carbohydrates. A ratio of forty percent carbs, thirty-five percent protein, and twenty-five percent fat may lead to less fat accumulation for you. Remember that the calorie total still needs to be higher than what you consume to maintain your body weight.

Chapter 5:
Practical Tips That Can Change Your Life!

So far the content discussed has focused more on the science of nutrition. Now we dive into the practical application of eating to gain weight. These were primarily learned by me from experimenting on myself and hundreds of clients while factoring in real-world variables such as time and money. Many tips were learned from various courses from some of the most respected people in the fitness industry, then applied in my own "lab," the gym, to see if they were practical. Some are very simple but may unlock a hidden variable within you that will end years of skinny frustration.

One of the simplest tips is to eat fast. When eating, your body releases a hormone called cholecystokinin (CCK) that tells you that you are full. Trying to stuff yourself beyond that point is miserable for most people. This hormone, however, is slow to be released. Eating fast allows you to consume more food before the hormone signals you to stop. On the flip side, those wanting to lose weight by eating less should eat slower and stop when eighty percent full. When eating fast to fullness and beyond, I think the protein portion should primarily be consumed first to insure that it goes down before you are full from the carbs and fats. Carbs tend to bloat your stomach more, especially as water is consumed with them. Be careful with the fast eating method and not look like Joey Chestnut, the hot dog eating champion, at the family Easter meal in the nice restaurant. Pick and choose your battles with the knife and fork so you don't have to battle with the family!

Now that you are full and can't eat another bite, it is still possible to consume good muscle building nutrients by drinking… no not beer, but rather a small protein shake, weight gainer, or chocolate milk. You can usually drink something even when you are full. These post-fullness cocktails don't have to be full servings. A scoop of weight gainer in a cup of water or milk can provide an extra 150–200 calories or a cup of chocolate milk could do the same. Do this with every meal five times a day and your daily total just increased by 1000 calories. This one trick may be enough to start gaining weight after being stagnant for years. If someone, regardless if they are trying to gain, maintain, or lose, is having trouble reaching the one+ gram of protein per one pound body-weight goal from food alone, simply adding 1 scoop of whey protein (~twenty grams) in one cup of water after each meal will increase their daily protein total by eighty to a hundred grams if they are eating four to five meals a day.

Other tips to get more nutritious calories include having a handful of mixed nuts between meals or chocolate-covered almonds for dessert. The amount of chocolate is small compared to the almond and they taste delicious. A handful (one ounce) supplies an additional 200 calories or so, and most of them will be from healthy monounsaturated fats. Fiber is also very high, and most of us could use a little more in our daily diets (at least twenty-five grams). Many who insist they are full and couldn't possibly eat another bite somehow always find a way to eat an ounce of chocolate almonds. Those on a fat loss diet could even have a few, not a few handfuls, to curb a sweet tooth craving since they are much more nutritious than malt balls or solid chocolate balls.

Peanut butter, or even almond butter, and honey on whole grain bread sandwiches are also a great dessert option or between meal snack. People often mistakenly classify peanut butter as a protein source when in fact it is much more of a fat source. It is not a great source of high quality protein or fat, so be sure to consume PB in addition to or between high nutrition meals and not substitute meals for it.

Another essential tip is to always eat before bedtime. This shortens the amount of time between meals. For example, if you finish your last meal at 6pm and you don't eat breakfast until 7am, you have gone thirteen hours between feedings. If you ate just before going to sleep at 10pm and ate again at 7am, you would have gone nine hours. Even better, if you awake in the middle of the night, have a protein or weight gainer shake ready to drink, then go back to bed. A constant supply of muscle building nutrients is what it takes to constantly stay in an anabolic (muscle building) state. Just remember to always follow the protein with every meal rule when consuming additional snacks that aren't part of a regular meal.

Many times the naturally skinny, hard gainer (ectomorph) simply needs more carbohydrates to stimulate growth. Often their metabolisms are very high and they burn off the primary source of fuel (carbs) as quickly as they are consumed. Their muscles and fat stores are used for energy because their gas tank is already empty. It's kind of hard to keep muscle gaining if it is used as a fuel source. An excellent and convenient trick to consume more calories is to eat several pieces of whole grain bread with your meals. Each slice contains roughly twenty grams of carbs, plus five grams of protein. Eat three to four slices with every meal four to five times a day, and your fuel tank will be full while your muscles will be spared. I have recently become a fan of Dave's Killer Bread. Each slice is packed full of organic nutrients and it is delicious!

Junk food, or shall we say "less than optimum nutrition food," can also play a role in gaining muscle. Some metabolisms are so high that they can't gain weight even after eating large nutritious meals six times a day. In cases like these, adding a slice of cake or ice cream for dessert is a great way to get extra calories that might be used as fuel for training while your healthier choices of protein, carbs, and fats may be spared for muscle building recovery. Adding a cup or pint of chocolate milk after your meals is an excellent "junk food" choice since it does have some additional protein (eight grams per cup) and it is liquid so can be consumed even when full from eating. A cup of chocolate milk after six meals will provide an additional 900 calories to your daily total! Some may be saying "that's a lot of sugar, too," and they're right. This isn't meant to be a habit for life, only for short periods while breaking through a plateau. If you see yourself accumulating too much body fat, then simply taper off the chocolate milk by a pint or two a week. The same goes for cake or ice cream.

Other extra calorie examples include pizza and cereal. Pizza gets a bad rap sometimes as a junk food choice, but I find it way better than doughnuts or beer. Sure it may not be a great choice for those trying to restrict their calories, but for adding muscle to a skinny frame, it isn't that bad. It at least contains protein, carbs, and fats where foods like doughnuts have virtually no nutritional value. You can make it even healthier by ordering a garden pizza packed with various veggies and adding chicken to it. Adding olives will also give you some good monounsaturated fats. Always try to include a healthier choice of meat and add veggies to it. My college weight gain dessert favorite was eating a bowl of Captain Crunch or other brand of cereal. Pop Tarts were also a good junk choice, and they were very portable as well. Cheeseburgers also get a bad rap. They have a load of protein from the beef, additional casein protein from the cheese, and a minimum amount of carbs from the bread. Making them yourself by choosing ninety percent lean beef, adding tomatoes and spinach, and whole grain buns can turn a society-labeled junk food choice into an excellent nutritious meal. Fast food burgers can be made much more nutritious too by not ordering fries, chips, or a soft drink with it. And don't forget the chocolate covered almonds or PB and honey sandwiches that we discussed earlier.

This doesn't give one the green light for uncontrolled junk food eating. Rationalizing it by saying you are "bulking up" is only an excuse to ignore the principles of good nutrition and convince yourself that your additional twenty pounds of fat is actually muscle. Some additional body fat is expected eventually when rapidly gaining weight, but it should be at a manageable level where modifying the diet and training can easily bring the levels back down. Those who stress over gaining a little fat while they are gaining muscle often start restricting the calories too much and muscle building stagnates once again. Keep the fat accumulation manageable, though, because trying to get lean after "bulking up" can be difficult, especially if you have become accustomed to eating badly the majority of the time.

The key is to not slide too far over where you are substituting the "junk food" for sound nutrition. It is always better to get extra calories from using the earlier mentioned strategies but the desserts can be used when you have already have consumed your targeted protein, carbs, and fat requirement.

Case Study: Monroe

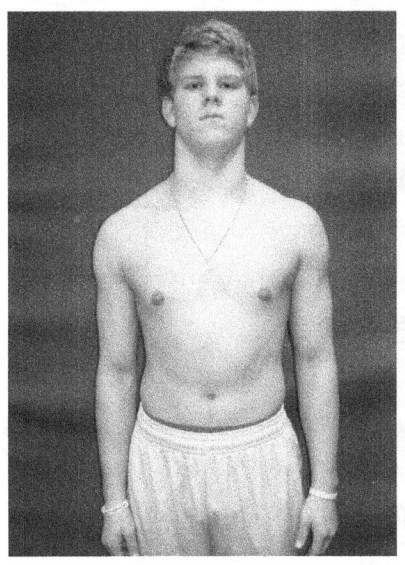 

Monroe, who had been training with me since he was a 130-pound eighth-grader, was 170 pounds in the first picture and had just suffered a football-related transverse process injury during his junior season in high school. He had been cleared to start lifting again a few months later. The initial workouts focused on performing movements that would strengthen his core and on beginning some light power work through jump/hop progressions and medicine ball progressions. The strength work for the lower body focused on single-leg strength to minimize the spinal load until a good base strength had been built. His diet was modified to increase his protein to 1.5 grams of protein a day, which proved to be a challenge since he had a low tolerance for post-workout protein/carb (weight gainer) shakes and would often throw up when consuming them. We tried various types of protein, both plant-based and animal-based, until he found one he could tolerate, then we had him consume fruit or whole grain bread, oatmeal, etc., for a carb source. We gradually introduced Olympic lifts back into his training. They were performed from the hang position to minimize the spinal torque. (All of our athletes perform Olympic lifts from the hang for the same reason, and the vast majority of athletic benefits come after pulling past the knees, plus they are much easier to coach to groups.) After a year of consistent training, Monroe was over 190 pounds in body weight and was hang cleaning 300 pounds with excellent technique. His parents are small framed, so he was able to greatly overcome less-than-optimal "get big" genetics to get to his size. He had a successful senior year of high school football and went on to play running back in college.

Chapter 6:
Pre- and Post-Workout Nutrition

What you consume immediately before and after training can have a significant impact on gaining muscle and recovering better for your next workout. A small pre-workout snack consisting of fifteen to twenty grams of protein and thirty to forty grams of carbohydrate will provide some energy and keep blood sugar levels high while training. While most of the fuel you will use for your workouts will come from stored carbohydrates and fats from yesterday's meals, the small pre-workout snack can have protein-sparing effects during your workout. In other words, your muscles are less likely to be tapped into for an energy source because there is sufficient fuel in the tank. A half sandwich, a scoop of weight gain powder, or a scoop of protein powder in diluted orange juice are simple examples. A more sophisticated pre-workout approach would be consume one of the previous examples thirty minutes to an hour prior to training, then consume ten to twenty grams of branch chain amino acids (BCAAs) in water immediately before lifting. The BCAAs are a much purer form of protein that will be immediately available in the bloodstream as muscle is being broken down during the training. This will minimize lean tissue lost and begin protein synthesis (repair) quicker. It would be an excellent idea to sip on BCAAs or a scoop or two of weight gain powder (protein plus carbs) during the workout as well as when trying to gain weight. Nutrition in liquid form is a better option in the immediate pre-, during, post-workout period due to its ability to be broken down more efficiently by the digestive system as well as providing some needed hydration lost during training. If you are training in an extremely hot and humid environment, adding a quarter or a half teaspoon of salt to your during-workout drink may also help to assist sufficient hydration.

Post-workout nutrition is even more critical for gaining mass. After a hard workout your body has broken down much muscle tissue (if the intensity was sufficient) and is in need of repair. The glycogen supplies have been used for energy and the tank is running on empty. Your body is like a sponge during this time, ready to soak up nutrients to replenish the tank and to start repair. The catabolic (tearing down) process is peaking and it's now time to switch to an anabolic (building up) state.

A post-workout recovery drink should consist of a ratio around two to one of carbs to protein. Generally speaking, for most women or smaller males this should be around forty to fifty grams of carbs and twenty to twenty-five grams of protein. Fat levels should be low in the post-workout drink to avoid slowing down the absorption rate of the much needed protein and carbs. Generally speaking, most males should have around sixty to eighty grams of carbs and thirty to forty grams of protein. Don't be too concerned if the ratio isn't perfect or the brand doesn't seem too scientific. In fact, some studies have shown that chocolate milk consumed as a post-workout drink outperformed several expensive brands in replenishing lost glycogen and initiating protein synthesis. The best thing about chocolate milk is its convenience. Every gas station or drug store sells it and nearly everybody likes the taste. It contains protein and carbohydrates in a decent ratio. Don't be alarmed about the high sugar content. Post-workout carbs need to be replaced fast, and simple sugars will be rapidly absorbed. However, chocolate milk is not as superior quality as a good protein/carb weight gain powder. The powders will most likely contain a higher protein content and a higher quality of carbohydrate than the sugar in chocolate milk.

Powdered post-workout formulas are disguised often as weight gain powders. Weight gain formulas are basically protein with carbohydrates added in a usual ratio of around two-to-one or three-to-one carb to protein. Post-workout drinks should NOT be just protein alone when trying to gain muscle. I often see this mistake made by athletes or adult trainees. Certain diets for trying to get leaner may call for protein alone, but most everyone needs to replenish the lost glycogen by the additional carbs. Some studies have shown that post-workout protein consumption is more efficient with the addition of carbs. Many people get a carb phobia and are scared to eat carbs for fear of gaining fat. They train hard for one or two hours and think consuming fifty grams of carbs in a post-workout drink will make them fat. As a result, their bodies use protein or their own muscle tissue as fuel, and end up storing body fat in a preservation mode. The post-workout window of one to two hours is an excellent opportunity for you to give your body well-deserved nutrients to help recover more efficiently.

Post-workout drinks can have a major drawback though. They can make you feel full where you won't want to eat. Most people, knowing that they need to refuel after a workout, plan to eat right after they train. The problem is that they just consumed a drink consisting of 300+ calories and they are full. The solution to this is to delay the post-workout drink. If you are going to be eating within thirty minutes after training, then eat first before having your drink. You can always drink when you are full from eating, but it is difficult to eat when full from your drink. The post-workout meal should be in similar ratios to the drink. Choose a good lean protein portion and a good starchy carb portion such as potatoes, rice, whole grain pasta or bread, pinto or black beans, etc. Try to keep the post-workout meal under ten percent fat. Now is not the time to eat the greasy burger or French fries. Your body is in a catabolic state and high octane nutrition needs to be delivered in this post-workout window. Eat fast to allow more food to be consumed before you get full, then consume the drink within an hour of finishing the meal. If you are going to stop by the store first or visit after your workout before going to eat and it's going to be more than thirty minutes after your last set, then consume a drink immediately following your workout and eat later. Still try to keep the post-workout meal within an hour or so though. I think also that the post-workout meal should be the largest meal of the day. In fact, post-workout nutrition is so important that I would rather someone skip a workout until later if they knew they were unable to eat or drink quality nutrients afterwards. For example, some school workouts or adult work schedules have 6am training then don't allow time for eating until lunch at noon. This puts the body in a catabolic state for too long and is counterproductive in building muscle and strength. If you are forced into this situation, then at least be prepared with a huge post-workout drink to quickly gulp down before class or work. This will hold you over until lunch, which should be another high carb with protein meal. Some schools or situations won't have a refrigerator or blender available. No problem. Just have your powder alone in a shaker bottle, add water, mix, and drink. Don't make excuses. Find solutions to these situations. Nobody said gaining muscle was easy.

An ideal pre-/post-workout weight-gain plan would be as follows:

1. Consume a small carb/protein meal one hour pre-training.
2. BCAAs (Branched Chain Amino Acids) right before lifting. Read label for suggested dose.
3. Sip on half serving of weight gain powder (protein/carbs) in water during training.
4. BCAAs immediately following training.
5. Wait twenty minutes to consume high carb/med protein/low fat meal or drink. Add five grams of creatine in the post-workout drink.
6. Take a twenty minute nap or go to bed.

Recently a few of my 150–170 pound teenage athletes did very well gaining weight by taking two scoops of weight gainer (twenty grams protein/forty grams carbs) in water before lifting then another two scoops in a pint of chocolate milk with five grams of creatine monohydrate added, immediately after their training.

Chapter 7:
Supplementation

In addition to the weight gain powders and BCAAs previously discussed, there are a few other essential supplements to consider when trying to gain weight. Protein powders can be helpful to insure that 1.0–1.5 grams per pound of body weight is consumed. Adding a mini shake consisting of a scoop of protein with every meal can easily add 80+ grams to the daily total when it may be difficult to consume that much extra in solid food. The same can be said with weight gain powders (protein + carbs) when trying to get additional calories. These powders can be easily mixed in water or in milk for additional calories. One scoop of powder in one cup of water can supply an additional 100–150 calories of muscle building nutrients. Be aware that most protein powders and weight gain powders provide around the same amount when the same size serving is used. Many labels boast that they contain much more protein or calories when in fact all that is bigger is the serving size. I remember some weight gain powders boasting "2000 calories per serving" when in reality the serving size would be two cups of powder and only five or so servings per large container. Try mixing two cups of powder in sixteen ounces of water or milk! Post-meal shakes don't have to be large to add some additional nutrients. If you are using the powders as a meal replacement, then make a large drink and add nutrients to it such as a handful of spinach, yogurt, banana, half cup of dry oatmeal, peanut butter, ice cream, or whatever you choose. A good rule to follow is to not have two consecutive drinks as part of meal replacement. Solid food has many nutritious properties that shakes may not have. Supplements are meant to do just that, supplement an already sound nutritional program.

Many people ask if they should mix weight gain or protein drinks in milk or water. Either one is fine for gaining weight. While whole milk contains more calories than two percent or skim milk, it also contains much more dairy fat. The drinks may be thicker and leave you more bloated than skim milk or water. Adding water to powdered drinks provides more hydration and may be easier to digest, leaving you ready for another meal sooner than a thick milk shake. Shakes made with milk will certainly have more protein and calories than ones mixed with water, so you may want to use less powder to get the same targeted nutrient value. This can be helpful if you're on a budget and need your can of powder to last longer. When I was in college and on a very limited budget (which we will discuss more in depth in the Poor Man's Eating chapter), I could take milk from the cafeteria back to my room after my meals. You couldn't take cartons, but you could fill up a cup. The cup I would bring with me was huge, probably forty-four ounces or so. I would leave it in my refrigerator until bedtime and mix it with a small amount of powder or at least have it by itself for extra nutrients.

Almond milk has gained popularity lately, but only use it if you are lactose intolerant. It has no protein and very few calories. Soy milk should be avoided, as high amounts of soy tend to increase estrogen levels, Not good when trying to build muscle that is dependent on high testosterone levels. Drinking chocolate milk all day long may not be the best idea either since the high sugar content may lead to excessive fat gain and sugar cravings. Personally if given a choice and a budget is not a factor, I would rather use water and add an additional scoop of powder to make up for the milk calories.

How much powder to use can vary on the situation. As discussed earlier, post-meal booster shakes can be very small. A serving of ten to fifteen grams protein and/or twenty to thirty grams carbs should be plenty if you ate enough at your meal. If you were unable to eat much, drink a larger drink. Drinks used as meal substitutes should aim for thirty to fifty grams protein and/or fifty to eighty grams carbs. Consider the size of your athlete when making these shakes. A 100-pound athlete's shake doesn't have to be 600+ calories to have an anabolic effect. A 220-pound athlete needs larger servings of course. Tailor your shakes to your needs, not by the suggested serving size on the labels.

Creatine is also a supplement that has been proven to work. It increases the ATP stores that can lead to more intense workouts. It also draws more water into muscle cells and can increase body weight as a result. A fully hydrated muscle is stronger, thus increasing the overall horsepower an athlete can produce. Creatine is found in red meat, so if you are already consuming large amounts of red meat, you may not see much of a boost since your levels may already be high. Suggested doses are five grams a day. Some recommend a high "loading phase," but I don't feel this is necessary or effective. Make sure you are getting plenty of water, at least two to three litres a day and more for hot, humid environments to avoid cramping or gastrointestinal distress. Also, it has been recommended by some experts to not take creatine until you are eighteen years old. Your kidneys are developing in the younger years and it is better to be on the cautious side. That being said, some have greatly exaggerated the harmful effects of creatine. It is not crack cocaine. It's a substance already found in smaller quantities in meat. When buying creatine, go with creatine monohydrate. Don't waste your money on fancier, highly marketed formulas. Five grams of creatine monohydrate added to your pre- or post-workout drink or with a cup of sugary sports drink will be just as effective in getting it shuttled to the muscles. I also think it's a good idea to cycle creatine. Take it for two months or so then lay off for a month or two. It stays in your system quite a while so you won't see a drastic drop in weight or performance. I don't value creatine near as much as I like protein or weight gain drinks, but it may give you a little extra boost.

It is also a good idea to take a daily multivitamin. Many people are marginally deficient in certain vitamins and minerals, and taking a multivitamin can insure that enzyme activity and other bodily processes run smoothly.

Fish oil should be consumed daily to provide the body and brain with good polyunsaturated fats. John Berardi recommends a balanced fat intake between one-third saturated fats (from meats and eggs), one-third monounsaturated fats (olive oil, avocado, nuts, etc.) and one-third polyunsaturated fats (salmon, walnuts, flaxseeds, etc.). Fish oil contains high amounts of Omega 3s, which have many positive health benefits such as anti-inflammation, heart health, improved insulin sensitivity, and cognitive function. Omega 6 has some positive benefits as well, but most diets contain way too many Omega 6s, which lead to increased inflammation. Processed foods, oils such as corn and canola, and many seeds such as sunflower seeds tend to push the Omega 6 ratio way out of balance. Many aching joints can be attributed to a high Omega 6/low Omega 3 ratio. I use small amounts of olive oil for a nonstick substance in my skillet when cooking eggs or ground beef. The harmful effects of free radicals from heating oil won't occur until it reaches the smoke point, so add all your food to the skillet before the oil starts smoking.

When buying fish oil, look for the ones highest in EPA and DHA. These are the active Omega 3 ingredients that provide the health benefits. Fish oil capsules generally are one gram each but the EPA/DHA amounts can vary significantly from brand to brand. Consume between one to three total grams daily of EPA/DHA (read the labels to see amounts) and try to eat wild-caught salmon when possible. Capsules are a convenient way to take fish oil, but bottled oils such as Carlson's can be very good and contain high amounts of EPA/DHA.

A powdered greens supplement is also an excellent idea to help get a recommended twelve daily servings of vegetables and fruits. When trying to gain weight, it is recommended that you should consume a three-to-one vegetable to fruit ratio. It is often difficult to get in twelve servings (nine veggies, three fruits) a day. Powdered greens are dried veggies and fruits condensed in a powdered form that can provide the benefits of two to three servings in a small scoop. These powders are also an excellent source of probiotics, which are essential in providing the digestive system with healthy bacteria. Add a scoop or two to your protein drinks to make them much more nutritious. When trying to gain weight, don't fall into the habit of eating only meat and starch. Overall and long term health should also be a concern. While fish oil, multivitamins, and greens powders may not directly budge the scale needle, you will be much healthier when you are gaining additional muscle. After all, it's hard to gain healthy weight when you are frequently ill or your joints hurt.

One popular supplement that I am not a fan of is an energy drink such as Red Bull or Monster. These drinks increase the heart rate, which exercise does also. It is not a good idea, in my opinion, to take a substance that artificially increases the heart rate prior to doing intense exercise, which further increases the heart rate. In hot, humid environments this can be even more dangerous. If you need your heart rate increased before you exercise, it would be much better to go through a brief dynamic warm-up that will also prepare your body for the intense exercise to follow. Nobody has ever had a problem with elevating their heart rate by doing a max effort one minute Airdyne or assault bike ride either.

RTD (Ready to Drink) post-workout drinks are numerous, but not many have a good two-to-one or three-to-one carb to protein ratio that optimizes glycogen replenishment and protein for repair. Most RTDs, such as Muscle Milk, are mostly protein and contain very few carbs. Muscle Milk Collegiate does have a good carb/protein post-workout ratio though. If these are your only options, make sure to eat some fruit or a source of complex carbs (bread, pasta, rice, potato, oatmeal, etc.) along with it to get somewhere near the desired ratio. A liquid source is always better because it can be broken down more rapidly by the digestive system but many compromises and modifications will have to be met when trying to gain healthy weight.

It is important to note that pre-/post-workout drinks are meant to be taken immediately pre- and post-workout. Carry them to the gym or practice and have them ready to go when you need them. It is too easy to get distracted by a conversation or "I need to run a few errands first" and not take them when you need them. Powders in the correct amounts can be kept in empty shaker bottles, ready to have water added when it is time to drink. Being prepared is vital to gaining muscle. Get used to carrying a small cooler with you and have it filled with prepared meals and snacks. Going long periods of time between meals is not optimum for gaining muscle, and it is too easy to be caught without good options. Tupperware containers can have meals in portions that you need instead of trying to stop at a convenience store and guess what to get. Pre-cook your meals so good quality protein sources are easily available.

People often ask me what brands to buy when supplement shopping for themselves or their kids. Don't get too overwhelmed with the choices. They are supplements, not magic potions. While some are certainly better than others, consistency in taking them and finding the correct nutritional ratios are going to be more important than a particular brand. Protein and weight gain powders are just broken-down food for convenience. There are hundreds of choices of them to choose from. Read the labels first. Skip the gimmicky claims on the front and go to the graph on the back that shows how much protein, carbs, and fats are in them. Next, look at the ratio of carbs to protein when selecting a weight gain supplement. Remember the two-to-one ratio of carbs to protein. If it has thirty grams of protein, it should have around sixty or so of carbohydrates. Don't worry if the ratio isn't exact. It most likely won't be. The biggest mistake I see when athletes buy them is that they buy protein powders that have very few carbs. This is fine if you are simply trying to add more protein to your meals but not as a primary pre-/post-workout drink. Remember, the recommendations in this book are primarily for those trying to gain weight. Taking fish oil, multivitamin, protein, and greens powder are also excellent for those trying to lose weight, but keep in mind that most reading this are trying to learn how to gain. Also, it is important to note that post-workout recovery drinks should be consumed after your sport practices as well. Weight lifting doesn't have to be involved to count as a workout. You are still burning high amounts of glycogen and breaking down muscle tissue, so follow the rules of nutrition we have discussed. The same goes for the timing of your next meal. If you will be eating within twenty to thirty minutes of your practice, save the drink for dessert instead of post-practice so that you won't be full and unable to eat.

Also, when looking at the labels be sure to check the serving size. Many will appear to be much higher in protein and calories when in fact all that is different is that the serving sizes are bigger. Remember to make your serving size according to your individual needs and body weight, not to what the label suggests. A 220-pound athlete's serving size is going to be larger than a 120-pound athlete's to achieve the desired effect.

While there are hundreds of brands to choose from and I am certainly not familiar with the majority of them, I do have a few favorites that I currently suggest. These seem to taste good to most people, and after all, few will drink them if they don't taste good. It is somewhat unfortunate to me that the taste of a supplement is the primary concern for many people. These are supplements, not ice cream. Take them for function first and taste last. These mix well and are not excessively expensive. Without getting into much detail, these are my current supplement brands I take or suggest to my clients:

1. Weight gain and pre-/post-workout powder:
    a. Muscle Milk Collegiate (This style has the two-to-one carb/protein ratio. Regular Muscle Milk doesn't. Make the right choice.)
    b. Cytogainer.
2. RTD (Ready to Drink) post-workout drink:
    a. Muscle Milk Collegiate
    b. Gatorade Recovery
    c. Chocolate milk
3. Protein Powder
    a. Designer Whey
    b. Hexapro or MP Combat Protein — both are good blends of five+ different proteins that are better choices for meal replacement than whey, when slower absorption is needed. If just adding extra protein to meals or for post-workout protein when fast absorption is needed, stick to whey if possible.
4. Creatine
    a. Monohydrate form
5. Fish oil
    a. Capsules containing 500+ active Omega 3 EPA/DHA
    b. Carlson's Fish Oil
6. Multivitamin
    a. Men's or Women's formula
    b. Vitamin D—for winter months of limited sun exposure
7. Greens Supplement
    a. Green Source Life Greens (or similar greens product)

8. Branch Chain Amino Acids
    a. MR (Muscle Recovery) by Infinite Fitness
    b. MS (Muscle Synthesis) by Infinity Fitness
9. Carbohydrate Powder
    a. Real Food by Rich Piana
    b. Waxy Maize
    c. Maltodextrin

Don't get too caught up in what brand but do choose higher quality supplements, which sometimes can be hard to tell by just reading the sales pitch. Order them online from places like Puritan's Pride or Bodybuilding.com and you will save many dollars over buying them at most health food stores. We will discuss other money saving suggestions in the poor man's eating chapter down the road. The important thing to remember about supplements is that they are meant to supplement an already optimal nutritional plan. The secret supplements that many ask me about that can have the most profound effect in strength, size, and performance are—get ready for this—groceries! They're legal, safe, and can be found in thousands of stores across the country. Learn to eat before spending money on supplements that won't work unless proper amounts and timing of protein, carbohydrates, fats, and water are consumed. Food can have drug-like effects on the body when properly utilized.

Another popular nutritional supplement is the protein bar. There are pros and cons with them. Generally speaking, the nutritional quality is not that great. They contain several preservatives to increase their shelf life. Hidden substances such as glycerol are often an ingredient and not included in the total carbohydrate amount on the label. The most damaging con in my opinion is also a pro. They are convenient. They can be easily taken anywhere and provide a protein source which doesn't have to be refrigerated. They can be carried on flights, to competitions as a source of nutrition during long breaks between games, while hunting or fishing, etc. The convenient pro can also lead to them being a con when good meals are skipped in favor of a bar because you were too busy to prepare one: It is easy to add up at the end of the day and see that you have consumed four bars and one or two meals. Daily preparation and carrying a small cooler packed full of chicken, rice, broccoli, almonds, and fruit is always a better choice than relying on bars. The nutritional value of a peanut butter and honey sandwich on whole grain bread with a scoop or two of protein powder or a big glass of milk is also a much better choice. That being said, bars can be used as desserts for extra calories and between meals when other food isn't available. I'm not suggesting that they should be eliminated, just don't get into the habit of making them a big part of your diet. A good rule with shakes and bars is to try to never have two in a row. Have solid meals between each one. They are supplements to use in addition to good nutrition. Don't fall into the convenience trap.

A factor to consider for those especially older than thirty-five is to have your testosterone levels checked by a doctor who is educated in this field. It is very difficult to gain muscle when testosterone levels are low. Normal testosterone levels are considered between 250-1100. However, symptoms of low T occur when levels are below 400. A doctor who is an expert in this field once told me he checked forty males over forty years old and thirty-nine of them had low T levels. Even males in their early twenties can have very low levels that they wouldn't know about had they not gone in for blood testing. Certain anabolic steroids that some have used for even a short time can suppress the natural testosterone production permanently. Free testosterone levels should also be checked because sometimes the overall levels are normal but the free levels (the amount available to be used) can be low. Women also should be checked to make sure they are in a normal range. The decision to use prescribed testosterone in normal ranges is a personal one. Some men don't like admitting that their manly levels are low, some think it goes against Mother Nature. A heart surgeon I train tells me it goes against Mother Nature while I tell him so does a mitral valve replacement. He tells me that the heart patients are dying and I argue that we all are, but some choose to live the last forty years of their life a fraction of their former selves. Low testosterone not only affects strength and muscle gains, it also affects depression, libido, energy levels, fat loss, and even osteoporosis. A good doctor or clinic that specializes in this area can monitor blood levels and keep you in normal ranges. This wasn't easily accessible twenty years ago but clinics are numerous now. It is a personal decision to make, but it sure is a lot easier to add muscle, strength, and lose body fat to a body in normal levels than one with the levels of an eight-year-old choir boy.

Chapter 8:
Poor Man's Eating

Unfortunately, most athletes that want to gain weight are usually struggling to make ends meet financially. They are either students with low paying jobs or their passion is in sports and not in making money. This presents a problem when you need to buy large amounts of food or supplements, but it is possible to still gain good weight on a limited budget.

Nutrient dense foods are those that are packed full of proteins, carbs, and healthy fats. Fortunately, many of these won't break the bank, especially if you make them yourselves. Foods like chili, lasagna, chicken and rice, and casseroles can be made in large pans and conveniently served over a period of several days or bought already prepared and just need some oven time to cook. Once prepared, simply cut a large portion and reheat in a microwave for easily accessible high calorie protein, carbs, and fats. The rest can be refrigerated for several days of convenient weight gaining meals. Pizza is another nutrient dense food that gets classified as junk food. Options such as veggie pizza with chicken added will be healthier than getting a greasy pepperoni. Mark Verstegen, the founder of EXOS, one of the top athlete-training companies in the world, used to suggest to his student athletes who skipped breakfast to eat a slice of leftover pizza for breakfast. It may not be the optimum choice, but at least they started their day with some protein, carbs, and fats.

Many people complain that healthy grocery shopping is expensive. I think the opposite. Compare the cost of a serving of oatmeal to a boxed, processed cereal and you will be amazed how much less expensive the oatmeal serving is. Protein sources can be cost efficient if you shop wisely. Canned tuna is inexpensive when purchased in large quantities from stores such as Sam's Club. It has a long shelf life and doesn't require refrigeration. Frozen chicken bought in bulk will also save you many dollars. Whole chickens provide several portions of protein and can easily be cooked in a crock pot while you're out doing other things. A pound of lean ground beef (ninety percent+) provides two to four servings and is not expensive when compared to a fast food burger. Eggs bought in large quantities are also inexpensive and can be used for extra protein when trying to make meats last longer. For instance, add two to three eggs to a quarter-pound of lean ground beef when cooking instead of using a half-pound portion. A quarter-pound portion of lean ground beef provides about twenty-three grams of protein and half pound has about forty-six. A quarter-pound with three eggs (a large egg has about six grams of protein so three would be eighteen grams) provides about forty-one grams of high quality muscle building protein that is much cheaper but also much more nutritious than a drive-through fast food breakfast. Another tip with eggs is to go ahead and eat the yolks. Yolks provide great protein packed with B vitamins and an egg white by itself is only about three grams of protein. The warning that the yolks raise cholesterol levels is flawed, as many factors such as genetics play a larger role in blood cholesterol levels than eating the yolks of a few eggs. Don't buy the cartoned egg-white choices either when trying to stretch your dollar.

Many grocery stores will greatly reduce the prices of their meats when their freshness dates are about to expire. This is a great way of saving money, and you can freeze them to make them last longer.

Starchy carbs, which as we have discussed should make up fifty percent of your diet if you are an ectomorph (skinny type) trying to gain weight, are very inexpensive if you know how to shop wisely. Rice, beans, potatoes, oatmeal, and pasta can be bought in large quantities for pennies per serving. As with all these recommendations, cooking them yourself is always going to be slightly cheaper than buying in a restaurant or even a fast food drive-through. Don't let the laziness of not wanting to cook be your excuse to say eating healthy is expensive. Cooking pasta is a matter of boiling water, putting the pasta in, and waiting until the noodles are soft. Pasta was my "go to meal" when I was in college. I would get large bags from discount grocery stores (the multicolored small noodles were my favorite plus I thought—wrongly—I might be eating healthier if they were colored like vegetables) along with several cans of cheap tuna. I kept a hotplate and a pan to boil water in my dorm room. A colander to drain the water, a can opener for the tuna, and a fork for my mouth was all I needed for my 10pm ritual. One of the best things about these starchy carbs is that they have a very long shelf life and require no refrigeration when uncooked. You can cook large quantities at a time, refrigerate them, and reheat in a microwave also.

Bread is also a good convenient starchy carbohydrate when trying to gain weight. It is easily transported and ready to eat. As

I mentioned earlier in the book, It can be added to meals to boost calories. The shelf life is shorter than the other starches mentioned and it may cost a little more per serving but it is still relatively cheap and convenient. Make sure to avoid white bread when buying, though, and stick to more whole grain varieties. Although gaining weight is your main priority, you must also take overall health in consideration and enriched white bread provides very little nutritional benefit.

A ten pound bag of potatoes can be extremely inexpensive when calculating cost per serving size. Even better, it is a natural unprocessed food source. The only downside is that they will have a shorter shelf life than rice or beans. Go in with a buddy and buy a large ten or fifteen pound bag if you are worried about some going bad before you consume them. Remember too that when I mention serving size that this only refers to the serving size suggested on the label, not for a hard gainer with high calorie demands. Your serving size may be two to four times what's on the label.

Pinto beans, black beans, kidney beans, black-eyed peas, etc., are all nutrient-dense carbohydrates that are also full of healthy fiber and extra protein. Sold in dry form, they are very cheap and have a very long shelf life. They do require more time to prepare and thus are not as convenient as other carb sources. You can always look for them as a side item on a menu or buy already cooked canned beans. Add them to burritos or salads when you are eating out.

Sometimes fibrous carbohydrates (green veggies, tomatoes, squash, spinach, broccoli, etc.) can be expensive just because they have a short shelf life and must be consumed quickly before they go bad. If you have concerns about this, buy large bags of frozen ones. They are much cheaper and will last much longer. You can heat water and cook them in minutes, and use only the portions you plan to eat. The same thing can be said for fruits. Blueberries and strawberries can last a long time frozen. Canned fruits (with no sugar added) and vegetables can often be found on sale. They may not be quite as healthy as fresh ones, but we are trying to gain weight on a limited budget and they will certainly be more healthy than eliminating them completely. Look for small home-grown produce stands found seasonally on the sides of busy roads in rural communities. Most will sell produce way cheaper than grocery stores and you will be supporting local farmers as well.

Healthy fat sources (don't forget about them!) can also be bought from wholesale grocers. Large bags of almonds or mixed nuts will have a long shelf life. Since most of you trying to gain weight will be on the ectomorphic body side (naturally thin), only about twenty percent of your total calories need to be from fats. With this in mind, a few handfuls a day of the nuts will make a large bag last a long time. A large bottle of olive oil can also last a long time. Avocados may only last a week so it may not be a great idea to buy large quantities of them. Don't bother spending extra money getting organic fruits and veggies. The jury is still out as to whether they make any significant difference other than on your pocketbook, and there have been several fraudulent cases of "organically grown" fields being sprayed with pesticides delivered from planes. If you become wealthy someday and want to buy all organic, then help yourself. Most people trying to gain weight will be better off using extra cash to buy more food instead of organic food.

Polyunsaturated fats such as fish oil supplements can be expensive if purchased from health food stores but can be much cheaper if bought online from companies such as Puritan's Pride.

Weight gain and protein powders, multivitamins, etc. are also much cheaper this way and will be delivered to your doorstep in a few days. This saves time and gas money also. Try your best not to buy supplements from health food stores such as ones found at your local mall. They are grossly overpriced compared to buying them online. When I was a teen trying to gain weight, it was difficult to find protein/weight gain powders other than in these stores (pre-internet days, too). Now you can find them in nearly all discount stores such as Target and Walmart. The prices are very good also. Again, don't be too concerned about getting a specific brand that your favorite bodybuilder endorses or one that you heard "my cousin Jimmy gained twenty pounds using Super Mass XXL" or whatever. Your concern should primarily be on ones that supply proteins, carbs, and fats to supplement your already sound nutritional plan learned earlier in this book.

    Bottled water is a waste of money if you are on a tight budget. Fill up empty bottles with tap water instead. A highly recommended idea for you college students is to get on your school's cafeteria plan instead of buying and preparing all of your meals. Most of the school cafeterias have designated times for breakfast lunch, and dinner. This is a great way to stay on a regular eating schedule. It is way too easy to say "I'll grab something after class" and then find that you have an empty refrigerator when it comes time to "grab" something. Most of the cafeterias will allow you to eat so much more food than you would if you were making a meal on your own. Most meal plans will save you hundreds of dollars in the long run, and you won't have to do the cooking. The variety of foods (salad bars, meat choices, etc.) will be far better than doing it yourself. The extra time you would've spent cooking can be used to study or sleep. You will also be far less likely to eat fast food, which won't be nearly as nutritious and will be much more expensive. Even more convenient, live on campus and choose a dorm close to the cafeteria. Eating is not just about protein, carbs, and fats. It can be a social event as well. You will be far more likely to meet great friends or potential dates by regularly eating in a school cafeteria every day than from sitting alone on your couch with a can of tuna and a couple of slices of bread. Just add a couple of extra meals or shakes to the three that you get from the cafeteria, and you should easily be able to get enough muscle-building nutrients in your daily diet. A great thing about being on the school cafeteria plan is that it forces you to eat even when you aren't hungry. You may not be hungry at 5pm but you know the cafeteria closes at 6pm. If you skip dinner, you risk becoming hungry later on ... not good when you are broke and the cafeteria doesn't open again until 6am the next day. Regular feeding times are good for both muscle gain and fat loss.

If buying protein powders for shakes is still out of your budget, then use the cafeteria to make your own shakes before bedtime. I was in this situation in college and would fill up a huge cup I brought with me with skim milk before I left dinner. I would buy the cheapest containers of oatmeal I could find and blend a cup of it with the milk before bedtime in my dorm room. A cup of dry oatmeal has about ten grams of protein, fifty-four grams of high quality complex carbs, and 300 calories. Adding it to the milk, you can easily get thirty to forty grams of protein and over 500 calories. A food processor that will make the oatmeal into oat flour (or just buy the oat flour if available) makes it mix even better than just the blender alone. Twenty years later I saw on a protein company's website where they now sell oat flour as a carbohydrate supplement. Guess being poor at the time and inventing oat shakes made me a weight-gaining scientist years ahead of my time! Depending on your cafeteria's policy about taking food home, you may be able to add an egg or banana, etc., to your poor man's shakes. I would often see the basketball players sneaking sandwiches or lunchmeat under their caps to have food for late night. One player in particular ended up being drafted in the first round of the NBA and is now on the NBA's fifty greatest players of all time list!

Case Study: Roli

Roli was a professional MMA fighter who was fortunate to make it to the UFC as a competitor on the show *The Ultimate Fighter*. After the show, he realized he needed to include functional strength/power training to his program, despite not being fond of lifting weights. He had always associated strength training with two-hour-long workouts that left you sore for days. A classic ectomorph with his long thin limbs and difficulty putting on muscle, Roli needed to gain muscle without going up in weight class (155 pounds). We added quality protein to his diet, making sure he got at least a gram of protein per pound of body weight, added two to three thirty- to forty-minute strength training sessions a week and also included the mobility, plyometrics, med ball, and sled progressions similar to those in the examples listed in this book. A pre-/post-workout protein/carb drink consisting of twenty grams of protein/forty grams of carbs was also a cornerstone of his training. His reps were kept in the three to five range generally to prevent a significant weight gain, but still allowed a good quality muscle gain. His brief but intense program still allowed him to train his BJJ, boxing, and wrestling without being worn out from a morning strength/power session.

Roli was able to significantly increase his strength/power with this program. He was able to greatly improve his muscle density, allowing him to still make weight at 155, cutting weight from 170 the five to six days prior to weigh-in. This allowed him to rehydrate back to 170 for his Saturday-night fights after Friday's weigh-in at 155. Prior to this program he would fight at around 160. Ten pounds of functional horse-power-producing muscle can be a great advantage in combative sports. The first photo here shows him weighing in at his first UFC fight at 155, and the other photo shows him a year later fighting at 170 but still weighing in at 155 as in the first photo.

Chapter 9:
Eating on the Go

Unfortunately, today's society makes sitting down at the dinner table three times a day a thing of the past. With our jobs, school, or family, we are constantly on the run. Trying to maintain a regular eating schedule may take more planning than usual. One solution is to cook in bulk so that you don't have much preparation time before each meal. Choose a day where you have some time to cook. For many people Sunday is a good day. Grill several servings of your protein sources, burger patties, chicken, etc., at one time. Get bags of spinach or chop large quantities of fibrous carbs. Bake several potatoes, cook several servings of rice, pasta, etc. for starchy carbs. Cook a large pan of pre made lasagna, chili, or chicken casserole. Slice several portions of roast beef, turkey, or ham. Make individual meals from these and store them in plastic containers ready to grab from your refrigerator. You can have an entire week's worth of meals with only an hour or two of Sunday preparation. Get a food scale if you want to be more precise with your serving sizes. A small cooler is essential to be able to carry two or three containers with you if refrigeration isn't convenient. You can also carry apples, oranges, nuts, sandwiches, bars, and other portable items in them so that you won't go long periods without food. This is also a great idea for game days or weekend competitions so that you don't end up settling for a hot dog or vending machine junk food when you get hungry and need optimum fuel for peak performance.

For most of us, fast food is always going to be at least a small part of our nutritional plan. It is unrealistic to think every one of your meals will come from a Tupperware container or a home cooked meal. Today's on-the-run lifestyle contributes to this but fortunately there are many more nutritious fast food choices available today than there were years ago. Most fast food places now have grilled chicken sandwiches available, whereas most only offered burgers and fries years ago. Some favorite fast food meals come from restaurants found nearly everywhere. McDonald's Egg McMuffins have 300 calories, eighteen grams of protein, and thirty grams of carbs (only three from sugar). Two of them with a carton of milk provides a good muscle building fast food meal. Many magazines such as *Men's Health* recommend them as a fast food breakfast option. Subway restaurants are even at many gas stations now. A footlong club, chicken, or roast beef loaded with spinach, bell peppers, cheese, onions, olives (for monosaturated fats), and cucumbers provides around fifty grams of protein along with starchy carbs from the bread and fibrous carbs from the veggies. Remember to lay off the soft drinks and chips or fries for the most part when eating fast food to keep your heart healthy and minimize excess fat accumulation.

Restaurants such as Chipotle and Qdoba are becoming increasingly popular Mexican-style eateries. They provide a choice of meat, rice, beans, veggies, and guacamole that can be great healthy fast food choices. For weight gaining purposes, get a burrito instead of a bowl since it will be much higher in carbs. Wendy's chili is packed full of good protein and carbs. Add a baked potato to it for additional carbs. They also serve grilled chicken sandwiches. Remember that, contrary to public opinion, a cheeseburger is not as bad for nutrition as you may think. It provides a good amount of protein and you can add tomatoes and onion to it for additional value. It's probably not a great idea to always choose burgers over other healthier options if getting them from fast food joints, as the protein/fat ratio will not be as healthy as your ninety percent+ lean home-cooked burgers. The additional fries and soft drinks contain very little nutritional value and give the burgers a bad reputation.

Perhaps the best option for eating out to gain weight is to choose a cafeteria when available. As with any meal, choose a protein source first, then a starchy carb source, then fibrous carbs. Add a roll, fruit, or dessert for additional calories. Get water to drink or unsweetened tea and don't get the extra calories from soft drinks. Advise those eating with you that are trying to trim up to take it easy on the starch and dessert! Most cafeterias provide good varieties of foods and some all-you-can-eat style allow you to get a ton of calories in. Be careful and don't go overboard with the limitless choices of sugary desserts though. Stick to the principles first.

Although the quest to gain weight for the skinny guy or girl requires a tremendous degree of consistent persistence, most do have a human side and will stray from course. What I'm talking about is that most will want to party from time to time. In the famous words of Tone Loc from the rap song "Wild Thing," "Hey you two, I was once like you and I like to do the wild thing!"

Consistent partying is inconsistent with athletic progress, but occasional partying within boundaries and modifications can be done without major effects on muscle building. This does not include the use of illegal drugs. These should be eliminated completely. Drinking is sometimes justified by those wanting to gain weight by thinking daily beers will give them extra calories. The calories from alcohol are void of any nutritional value, so get that thought out of your head. Drinking every weekend will do nothing but halt your progress as well. Alcohol in excess will lower your testosterone levels, dehydrate you, and effect the muscle-building anabolic environment that you have been working hard to achieve. It can suppress your appetite as well, which even for a day or two is not good for the ectomorph. My fall semester of my sophomore year in college, I, like many other students, found myself going to a couple of parties a week and having four to six beers at each one. I realized that despite my extreme dedication in the weight room, I did not gain any weight that I desperately wanted that semester. Only after I stopped did my metabolism get back on track and I started growing again. I would still go to the parties, but I wouldn't drink. I would still go to a club on a Saturday night (once I turned twenty-one), but I would order water or cranberry juice. I was able to gain muscle, have fun, and never had to worry about a DUI either!

    I know most will drink from time to time. There are ways to minimize the damage and keep the anabolic process going. Even if you don't drink, limit going out to one night a week. If you do go out, set a deadline to leave, like midnight or 1am. This will keep you on a reasonable sleeping and eating schedule as opposed to staying out until 4am and sleeping most of the next day. If you do sleep a lot longer than you usually do, then set your alarm for 8am or so and get at least a protein/carb drink or a light breakfast before going back to sleep for a few hours. If you do choose to drink, limit this to one night a month or less. If you are under twenty-one, don't drink at all since it is illegal but I know this is unrealistic for most nineteen-year-old weightlifting young men. If you do drink, don't get hammered. Only bad things happen after two beers, including DUIs, public drunkenness, fights, and saying things you regret later. Still try to stick to the eat-every-three-hours rule by ordering a club sandwich, slice of pizza, or chicken tenders from the bar. After you leave the party, don't go to bed without eating first and rehydrating with water. Look for twenty-four-hour restaurants such as Waffle House, IHOP, or Denny's. Follow the "choose a protein first" rule when ordering. If nothing is open, find a convenience store. Most of them now sell protein bars or Muscle Milk drinks whereas a few years ago this was unheard of.

If they are available, look for a protein source like milk, jerky, or a sandwich. Choose other foods after your protein like almonds, bananas, or even Pop-Tarts. Pop-Tarts aren't the worst junk food in the world and often can be used to keep calories up. If you are feeling depleted, eat some ice cream with your protein source. The important thing to remember for an ectomorph trying ot gain weigh is that junk food is better than no food at all. Be sure to drink at least a pint of water also. The best option when going out is to bring a small cooler with you and leave it in your car. Have it full of good choices ready to go. Turkey sandwiches, protein drinks, apples, etc. Take fifteen minutes from the club and go refuel then go back in and enjoy yourself! And besides, you don't want to be walking around in the club with flat, decarbed muscles after you've worked so hard to build them!

The day following your (hopefully) rare binge, get back to good clean eating principles. Make sure you hydrate (with water, not more beer) especially well and take a multivitamin as you should be doing anyway. Choose good lean protein sources and perhaps an additional fresh fruit. It would be a good idea to do a brief high rep and light workout or body-weight circuit. This will help rid your body of the toxins by pumping oxygenated blood throughout your system. Drink some Gatorade or other electrolyte drink and perhaps add a pinch of salt to it to help the rehydration process. It's not a good idea to do a heavy strength workout following a night of heavy boozing since the risk of straining or tearing a dehydrated muscle will be greater.

Adding muscle to a skinny ectomorphic frame isn't easy. If it were, everyone would be able to just will more muscle on their body. However, it is not as difficult as people think if you are willing to be consistent with eating and training. You must EAT, and EAT BIG! Eating the same amount as you have been and hoping that it suddenly starts working is idiocy. No training program in the world will work if not enough food is being consumed. Consistent efforts with the knife and fork are just as important as they are with barbells and dumbells. Fortunately, the power of food can have drug-like effects on the body when used properly. Gaining muscle to a naturally thin physique is like changing one's DNA. It takes consistency and persistence. I have provided a nutritional path that takes out the guesswork. Eventually, you will find what method works best for you and narrow your nutritional approach even more. Sometimes it can be as simple as adding two pieces of whole wheat bread to your five feedings a day. This provides an additional 1000 calories, 200 grams of complex carbs, and fifty grams of protein. Sometimes it takes a more detailed plan. Find what works for you while still sticking to sound nutritional principles discussed in earlier chapters. The same can be said about training, which we will dive into in the next section of this book.

Chapter 10:
Strength and Speed Development

Designing a Program

It is one thing to develop a plan to gain weight just for looks. It is another to develop one that will also make you a better athlete. Many other factors besides lifting weights are involved to insure one does not become "muscle bound." Describing the complete training plan in detail would involve a separate book. Instead, I will briefly cover the principles and refer you to a few excellent sources that cover them in great detail. I highly recommend purchasing Mike Boyle's *New Functional Training for Sports* and *Every Day Is Game Day* by Mark Verstegen. These two books will guide you through the steps needed to improved athleticism, regardless of whether or not you are trying to gain weight. Together, with the strength/hypertrophy section in the weight room that will be covered here, you will avoid the pitfalls of nonfunctional hypertrophy that happens too often with a poorly designed program.

The first component of a training day that should be addressed is soft tissue management. Muscles can easily get trigger points and small adhesions that interfere with normal function. If part of a muscle belly is of normal pliability and another part is contracted even at rest, the muscle can't function properly or optimally. Five minutes or so of foam rolling or trigger point pressure using a lacrosse ball prior to a workout will help the tissue and prepare it for stretching. Increased sessions of foam rolling will make the rolling more pain-tolerable as the tissue quality becomes better. It is also a great idea to do tissue work on regeneration days or post workout. Keep a tennis ball in your luggage when traveling if you're short of room when packing. There are many pictured examples of tissue management for the entire body in both of the books mentioned previously.

Mobility/flexibility is the next component that should be addressed. While gaining weight, it is important to maintain and improve your mobility of the ankles, hips, and thoracic spine. If those joints are not able to move thorough a normal range of motion, the joints that provide stability (knees, lumbar spine) are at a greater risk of injury. Flexibility of the muscles should be worked on to insure the added muscle tissue from gaining weight is properly lengthened and not at a greater risk of strains or pulls when participating in high speed moments on the field or court. Mobility and flexibility exercises performed after foam rolling can be managed in five to ten minutes once you have a routine in place.

The next area of the workout should emphasize strengthening and activating the core, or pillar. This involves the muscles of the torso and hips that are used in all athletic movements. Power is generated from and through the core, which also aids stability. Inefficient movements as a result of a weak core will result in decreased performance and an increased risk of injury. Progressive versions of planks, side bridges, glute bridges, and band movements that target the glute medius and hip flexors are covered in great detail in Boyle and Verstegen's books. They should be performed to strengthen these areas and to activate and prepare the body for the dynamic warm-up and movement/speed portion of the workout.

The dynamic warm-up is a series of movements performed over a ten- to fifteen-yard area that prepares the body for higher speed movements. It activates the nervous system, increases the heart rate while raising the core temperature, and coordinates the body as it will be used in sport settings. The dynamic warm-up can be broken down into linear movements for straight ahead speed days or lateral movements for multidirectional emphasis days.

After you have gone through the dynamic warm-up, you are now ready for plyometrics. While the previously mentioned soft tissue work, mobility/flexibility/pillar/core prep, and dynamic warm-up may seem like a lot, it can be efficiently completed in twenty-five to thirty minutes. Plyometrics bridge the gap between strength acquired in the weight room and speed on the field or court. Lower body plyometrics are composed of jumps, hops, and bounds while upper body plyometrics consist primarily of medicine ball throws. The movements of the medicine ball throws involve pushing, rotating, and overhead throwing. Medicine ball throws can be looked at as Olympic lifts for the torso. In fact, lower and upper body plyometrics can be substituted (although not as good, in my opinion) for Olympic lifts when the lifts can't be properly performed. Plyometrics should be performed in progressive stages and low repetition/high quality. The stages, usually lasting three to four weeks, should involve no more than around twenty-five foot contacts and throws per day. A typical phase one plyometric program may consist of three to four sets of five box jumps paired with three to four sets of eight med ball throws. Like the dynamic warm-up, emphasis on linear plyometrics and lateral plyometrics should addressed on alternating days. Boyle's book gives great instruction of the progressive stages.

Improving Speed While Gaining Weight

Training to "get big" is nothing new of course. What may be new to you are some of the methods used to get bigger while improving athletic performance at the same time. Many mistakenly associate a larger, more muscular athlete to automatically be better than his or her smaller competition then realize they may "look like Tarzan but play like Jane." Traditional bodybuilding programs that employ bodypart days often lead to nonfunctional hypertrophy (muscle growth). This means that while the overall size of the muscle is bigger, many of the gains are not in the contractile elements of the muscle. The gains don't transfer over to a higher production of force that is needed for improved athleticism. As we discussed in the beginning of this book, it's like adding 500 pounds to a car but not doing anything to the engine. The car may look stouter, but the extra weight actually decreases the overall horsepower. There are ways to gain weight while increasing horsepower for improved athletic performance. Speed improvements or increased vertical jump measurements aren't always necessary to indicate improved power. If an athlete gains thirty pounds and his times or vertical jump (VJ) remain the same, he/she is actually able to produce more horsepower than before. Imagine the decrease speed or VJ you would experience if you were to add thirty pounds of weighted vests while being tested. This is another example of nonfunctional hypertrophy. Improved speed and VJ (or broad jump, med ball toss, etc.) while gaining weight is an even bigger improvement in horsepower. This is assuming that the athlete is lean to begin with. The quickest way to improve speed and power for a nonlean athlete is to lose unnecessary body fat. Lineman in training for the NFL combine often lose some body fat (most have enough extra to lose) to make them faster. Again imagine running a forty-yard sprint with a twenty-pound vest (representing fat) versus without the vest. Once the combines are over and they want more weight to improve their leverage on the line, they can put the extra pounds of fat back on. Many skill position players that are extremely lean and light going into combine training may try to gain a few pounds of functional muscle to improve their horsepower and thus improve their speed and VJ. The type of training you perform to gain weight is critical to insure the additions are not "all show and no go."

It is important to realize that most all team sports are fast-twitch dominant. Most have more similarities than they do differences. Most involve sprinting, deceleration and change of direction, strength and power. The acceleration involved in trying to beat out an infield single is no different than when running a fast break. Acceleration in short distances at five to twenty yards is used much more than a forty- or hundred-yard dash. Seldom does an athlete run more than ten to twenty yards without having to change directions. We must train these common components to improve performance regardless of what team sport it is.

Legendary Canadian sprint coach Charlie Francis believed in spending as much time possible training the fast-twitch characteristics that his athletes possessed. We are born with a certain percentage of fast-twitch fibers (those important in sprinting, jumping, and throwing) and a certain percentage of slow-twitch fibers (those important in endurance events like long distance running, biking, and swimming). We also have intermediate fibers that can take the characteristics of either fast or slow twitch depending on how they are trained. This is especially important in the athlete's developmental years around ages twelve to sixteen. If you train fast twitch, these fibers will act more as fast twitch. Most great team sport athletes will not excel in training runs such as a mile because the fast-twitch qualities that make them great would be a liability in endurance events. I remember seeing defensive back Champ Bailey intercept Tom Brady and return it 100 yards for a touchdown. He was exhausted afterward and required oxygen on the sidelines. That doesn't mean he was out of shape; after all he was an elite player in the NFL. It rather showed that the vast majority of his training and playing involved short distances of ten to thirty yards because that's what ninety-nine percent of his position play involved. Had he spent a lot of time training to run 100+ yards, he may not have been as efficient at his position and ended up being an average player as a result.

Hall of Fame running back Earl Campbell would come in last place in his team's (Houston Oilers) one-mile conditioning test. When his coach Bum Phillips was asked by the media if he was concerned about his best player being last, Bum replied, "I guess we won't give him the ball when it's fourth and a mile." Campbell could have spent a lot of time training for the mile test and might have lost some of the speed and power that made him one of the greatest running backs of all time.

The message to remember for an athlete training to gain weight is to sprint and not distance run. Sprinting should be performed two to four times a week while gaining weight. This will insure that the gains made will adapt to the training stimulus of strength and power. As you get stronger and more powerful, these gains will transfer to speed. If you were to gain twenty pounds then start sprint training, it is unlikely that speed improvements will be significant and more likely you will be slower.

The volume of sprints should be low but the intensity high. Six repetitions of maximum-effort sprints of ten to twenty yards with sufficient recovery (thirty to sixty+ seconds) between reps should provide the training stimulus needed. Distance of maximum sprints do not need to exceed twenty yards because of the increased risk of hamstring pulls and the fact that most team sports' straight-line runs will be less than twenty yards. Speed development should be done over three to four progressive phases lasting three to four weeks each. Phase one emphasizes form and pushing the ground away while phase two and three increase the length, intensity, and competitiveness. Excellent explanations of these phases and drills are in Mike Boyle's book. It is important to note that multidirectional sprinting should be included as well since most of the movements in team sports involve change of direction. Sprinting in sports is rarely performed for distance more than ten to twenty yards without deceleration and change of direction. It is a big mistake to only train straight-line speed or train for the forty-yard dash as many speed coaches overemphasize. I have become a fan of testing my athletes every two weeks (sometimes even every linear speed day) throughout each training phase in a laser-timed ten-yard sprint. The personal bests are recorded and the athlete has three to four attempts every two weeks to beat their best times. The most important benefit to this is it insures a maximum effort. Athletes try their best to beat their personal best or beat a teammate. Flying starts can also be tested for top-end speed emphasis. There is little risk of hamstring strain with timed max-effort ten- to twenty-yard sprints, so keep the distance short. Typical speed development drills are often done at eighty to ninety percent even though 100 percent is coached. Laser timing with objective results insures that 100 percent effort will be given. To get fast, you have to train fast, and laser timing is excellent for producing 100 percent effort. Thanks goes to Steve Bunker of Mike Boyle Strength and Conditioning for this excellent strategy!

Some may question how gaining weight can improve speed. Remember that most that have trouble gaining weight will be ectomorphs (naturally thin). If you are gaining muscle while you are functionally strength/power training in the weight room and performing the sprints as we covered, you will be improving your horsepower with the additional muscle. Increased horsepower will lead to increased speed.

Sled pushing may be the most valuable tool for developing speed. While it may not do much for top-end speed, it is great for acceleration. Most sprinting in sports is acceleration dominant due to the short distances involved. Sled pushing provides an excellent sport-specific action that mimics the torso angle and pushing the ground away concept of using power to accelerate. Distance should be kept short, usually ten to fifteen yards. The amount of weight should not be so great that ten yards can't be covered in ten seconds or less. Progressive phases consist of three to four weeks of four to six reps of heavy sled marches followed by three to four weeks of lighter sled sprints. Phase three may include complexes consisting of a sled march followed by a maximum-effort sprint without the sled.

Sled pushing also helps develop the core and shoulder stabilizers. Specific weight is dependent on the friction provided by the surfaced being pushed on. In the South where I train, humid days make the sleds feel much heavier. Don't be overly concerned about increasing weight each week. Do a rep and add or subtract depending on the feel or the ten-yard/ten-second rule.

Case Study: Thomas

Thomas went from 150 pounds to 168 pounds after doing a ten-week program very similar to the three-day program described in this book. He learned correct technique first then added 5+ pounds to his lifts each week. He modified his diet by greatly increasing his calories and paying particular attention to increasing the quality of protein he consumed. Lean beef, chicken, fish, and eggs replaced his usual fast food choices. He also began consuming a post-workout drink that consisted of thirty grams protein/sixty grams carbs and made sure he ate an additional meal before bedtime. After gaining his functional weight, he was able to complete basic training with the US Army and be at the top of his class in the fitness tests, proving that his muscle gain was not "all show and no go."

Chapter 11:
The Weight Room

Resistance programs are necessary to insure the weight you gain is good functional muscle that will improve performance as well as build a larger physique. Simply eating more food without doing a well-planned progressive resistance program seldom results in functional weight gain. The body must have a reason to "hang on to the food" so that the food "sticks to the bones." The muscles grow larger by adapting to the specific demands you put on it. When you are giving great consistent effort in a well-designed training program, then you have a chance to grow. If your nutrition is equally as good, your odds greatly increase.

I have found over the years of training athletes that the most critical obstruction to gaining weight is not eating enough. Many come up with fancy programs involving complex time under tension or reps/sets schemes but no matter how great the program is, if there aren't enough nutrients being consumed it will be wasted effort. So many athletes are underfed because their caloric intake does not meet or exceed their caloric expenditure from exercising and overall metabolism. Once they find the right calorie range many begin rapidly gaining previously starved muscle.

The three- and four-day training examples I have provided may seem simple, but they will work greatly for most people trying to gain weight. If they follow the nutritional guidelines I provided earlier, most thirteen- to eighteen-year-old athletes could use a single example of this program for several years and gain a lot of performance enhancing/horsepower producing functional muscle. It is not uncommon to see a young athlete go from 130 pounds or so to 190+ pounds over their high school years by following a similar program ... if they are consistently eating and training well. As they become more experienced in the weight room (usually three+ years) they may need to tweak the basic program to keep gaining.

Most basic programs consist of three- to four-week blocks of a hypertrophy phase, strength phase, and power phase. There is nothing wrong with that for most athletes trying to gain weight if their nutrition is adequate. Since gaining weight is the primary emphasis of this book, the program examples I have provided are simplified even further by consisting of only two blocks of hypertrophy and strength. The main variation between the two blocks is just a greater emphasis on higher volume (primarily higher reps/time under tension) in the first four-week phase (hypertrophy) and a greater emphasis on strength (primary lower reps/higher loads) in the second four weeks. Although there is no "power" phase included, power is worked on every week in the form of plyometrics, sprints, and the power movements in the weight room (hang cleans, hang snatches, and one-arm DB snatches).

The program samples I present are different from typical weight-gaining bodybuilding programs. Typical bodybuilding programs have body-part days where "leg day" or "chest/triceps day" is worked usually one day a week for a high volume of sets and several exercises per body part. In my three- and four-day programs, the volume per movement (not muscles, even though the muscles are greatly being worked) is less, but the movements are worked several times a week instead of once a week. The fewer number of sets allows for quicker recovery so waiting a week to stimulate the same muscles is not necessary. Several studies have also shown that this lower volume/higher frequency approach produces greater results as well. Athletes doing this type of program typically report a mild soreness the day following a workout instead of "I couldn't walk normally for four days." This is important while sport-specific practice is being integrated with weight training. Practicing your sport while being greatly under-recovered is a recipe for injury and unproductive workouts and of course risks getting both the athlete and strength coach in the head coach's doghouse.

Variation of reps in the program is more important than variation of exercise selection, although most do the opposite. The trainer usually gets bored with the program before the athlete does. The trainer learns something new from a course recently attended or sees a new cool exercise on the internet and feels compelled to fit it into the athlete's program. Stick with the basics and change the reps every four weeks or so instead of "throwing the baby out with the bathwater." Too many times the sound basic program gets altered so many times that it gets away from the "meat and potato" exercises that are so valuable in development. I remember reading a quote from Bob Alejo, a famous American strength coach, just before the Beijing Olympics that said something like "I'm watching the best athletes in the world train and they are squatting, snatching, benching, inverted rowing, doing pull-ups, etc."

Once an athlete has been following a good sound program for three or four years and they seem to have hit a plateau in gaining muscle, then they can tweak the program a bit. Often the dilemma is how to program a system that is conducive to gaining mass, which often involves higher sets and reps (volume), while improving the strength and power (typically lower volume/higher intensity) needed for athletic development. While higher volume programs (typically bodybuilding type) may be good for gaining muscle, they usually don't do much to improve strength/power and you may end up with an athlete that is "all show/no go" or "looks like Tarzan/plays like Jane."

One of my favorite solutions to this problem involves performing a basic strength building exercise followed by an isolation bodybuilding type exercise. For example, a heavy set of five rep bench presses immediately followed by a slow set of dumbbell or cable flies for eight to ten reps. A lower body example would be a set of five TBDL (trap bar deadlifts) followed by a slow set of walking lunges for fifteen yards. A pulling example may be a heavy set of five chin-ups followed by a set of eight to ten inverted rows. The second exercise should immediately follow the strength exercise. This system allows for the strength component to be worked on while pairing it with a more isolated movement and gives the increased TUT (time under tension) that is conducive for hypertrophy. It is important that the isolated exercise emphasize the eccentric (lowering) part of the lift for a count of three to five seconds and not just done rapidly or with too much weight. As always, the power movements (cleans, snatches, etc.) should still be done prior to the strength/hypertrophy pairs to insure maximum power efforts in an unfatigued state and to promote excellent technique.

Another method that works well for improving hypertrophy while also gaining strength is the use of cluster sets. Clusters have many variations but one method that I have successfully used with many athletes involves doing a heavy strength exercise set followed by a fifteen- to thirty-second rest, then performing a few more reps followed by another brief rest, then finishing with a few more reps. A bench press example would be to do a heavy set of five, rack the weight and rest for fifteen seconds, do two to three more reps then rack it again and rest another fifteen to thirty seconds, then getting a few more reps. This is an intense method that should only be used for a few sets (one to two) and for only three to four weeks at a time. The same can be applied to TBDL (although be careful that correct form isn't compromised), chin-ups, etc. It is a great way to get stronger as well as increase the TUT that may be needed to break through a weight gaining plateau. Make sure you have a spotter on the bench press because you will often "hit the wall" and not have another rep left in you. Rolling a loaded bar down your body is no fun, and we've all made that mistake once in our youth.

Chapter 12:
Three- and Four-Day Examples

Three-Day-a-Week Basic Program

Weeks 1–4

Monday
    Power
    Anti extension

    Double leg knee dominant
    Vertical pull

    Straight leg hip dominant
    Vertical press

Conditioning

Wednesday
    Power
    Lateral stability

    Horizontal press
    Single leg knee dominant

    Horizontal pull
    Bent knee hip dominant

Friday
Power
Anti rotation

Double leg knee dominant
Vertical pull

Knee/hip dominant flexion
Hybrid press
Combine push–pull–core

Week 5

Deload
Do fewer sets.
Go a little lighter if needed.

It's best to pair your exercises. For example, perform one set of a power exercise, then perform one set of anti extension. After the desired sets are completed, move to the next pair.

Three-Day Basic Program: MONDAY

Monday	Weeks 1–4	Week 5	Weeks 6–9	Week 10
Hang clean	3x5	Deload	3x3	Deload
Pillar bridge	3x :20 holds	All exercises are performed for 1–2 sets instead of the usual 3	Rollouts (start with stability ball for 3 weeks before going to ab wheel) 3x6–9	All exercises are performed for 1–2 sets instead of the usual 3
TBDL (trap bar dead lift)	3x8–10		3x5	
Chins	3x8–10 or AMRAP (as many reps as possible) less than 8		Add weight if possible 3x3–5	
SLDL (single leg dead lift)	3x8–10		3x5	
½ kneel curl press	3x8–10		3x5	

Paired Exercises. The shading in each table shows which exercises to pair together. For example, perform one set of a power exercise (like the hang clean in the table above) then perform one set of anti extension (like the pillar bridge above). After the desired sets are completed, move to the next pair (the unshaded pair above, etc.).

Three-Day Basic Program: WEDNESDAY

Wednesday	Weeks 1–4	Week 5	Weeks 6–9	Week 10
1 arm DB snatch	3x5	Deload	3x3	Deload
Side bridge	3x :20 holds	All exercises are performed for 1–2 sets instead of the usual 3	1 arm farmer's carry 3x15 yards	All exercises are performed for 1–2 sets instead of the usual 3
Bench press	3x8–10		3x5	
Split squat	3x8–10		Rear foot elevated split squat 3x5	
Inverted row	3x8–10		1arm DB row 3x5	
BLHE (bent leg hip extension)	3x8 :05 holds		BLHE progression 3x5 :05 holds	

Three-Day Basic Program: FRIDAY

Friday	Weeks 1–4	Week 5	Weeks 6–9	Week 10
Hang clean or snatch	3x5	Deload	3x3	Deload
Kneeling palof press	3x8	All exercises are performed for 1–2 sets instead of the usual 3	Squatting palof press 3x8	All exercises are performed for 1–2 sets instead of the usual 3
Goblet squat	3x8–10		3x5	
Parallel grip chins	3x5–10		3x3–5	
2 leg slideboard leg curl	3x8–10		3x5 1 leg slideboard leg curl	
Alternate incline DB press	3x8–10		3x5	
Renegades	3x8–10		3x5	

Weeks 5 & 10
Can 1 rep max on Bench, Chinup, and Hang Clean on week 10.

Deload notes: If you are consistently training and the intensity is high, then it may be beneficial to take a deload week to allow the body to catch up to the training. If you are still learning technique and the intensity is low, then a deload week is not needed. If you have to miss a few days, then a deload week is not needed. Aging athletes may benefit more from deloading.

Four-Day-a-Week Basic Program

A. All movements get worked 2x week
   1. More total volume
   2. More anabolic stimulus and post workout feeding opportunities

Monday
  Power
  Anti extention

  Double leg knee dominant
  Vertical pull

  Single leg knee dominant
  Horizontal pull

Thursday
  Power
  Anti rotation

  Knee dominant, single leg
  Horizontal pull

  Knee dominant, double leg
  Vertical pull

Tuesday
  Power
  Anti lateral

  Horizontal press
  Hip dominant, straight leg

  Vertical press
  Hip dominant, bent leg

Friday
  Power
  Flexion

  Incline Press
  Hip dom/knee flexion

  Horizontal press, close grip
  Hip dominant, straight or bent

Wednesday/Saturday Regeneration day options
  Sleds
  Meditation
  Whirlpool
  Prehab hip/shoulder
  Cardio
     15-20 mins of low intensity
  Soft tissue/mobility

  Pool
  Arms
  Diaphragmatic breathing
  Massage
  Audio
     Ocean wave
     Rain

Four-Day Basic Program: MONDAY

Monday	Weeks 1–4	Week 5	Weeks 6–9	Week 10
Hang clean	3x5	Deload	3x3	Deload
Pillar bridge	3x :20 holds	All exercises are performed for 1–2 sets instead of the usual 3	Bodysaw 3x8–10	All exercises are performed for 1–2 sets instead of the usual 3
TBDL (trap bar dead lift)	3x 8–10		3x5	
Chins	3x8–10 or AMRAP if less		3x5	
Split squat	3x8–10		Rear foot elevated split squat 3x5	
1 arm DB row	3x8–10		3x5	

Four-Day Basic Program: TUESDAY

Tuesday	Weeks 1–4	Week 5	Weeks 6–9	Week 10
1 arm DB snatch	3x5	Deload	3x3	Deload
½ Turkish getup	3x5 each side	All exercises are performed for 1–2 sets instead of the usual 3	½ Turkish getup with glute bridge 3x5 each side	All exercises are performed for 1–2 sets instead of the usual 3
Bench press	3x 8–10		3x5	
SLDL (single leg deadlift)	3x8–10		3x5	
½ kneel curl press	3x8–10		3x5	
BLHE (bent leg hip extension)	3x8 :05 holds		BLHE progression 3x5 :05 holds	

Four-Day Basic Program: THURSDAY

Thursday	Weeks 1–4	Week 5	Weeks 6–9	Week 10
Hang clean or snatch	3x5	Deload	3x3	Deload
Tall kneel palof press	3x8	All exercises are performed for 1–2 sets instead of the usual 3	Split stance palof press 3x5	All exercises are performed for 1–2 sets instead of the usual 3
1 leg squat variation	3x 8–10		3x5	
Parallel grip chins	3x8–10 or AMRAP if less		3x5	
Goblet squats	3x8–10		3x5	
Inverted row	3x8–10		3x5	

Four-Day Basic Program: FRIDAY

Friday	Weeks 1–4	Week 5	Weeks 6–9	Week 10
Jump squats	3x5 with 10–20 lb vest	Deload	3x3	Deload
1 arm farmer carry	3x15 yards each side	All exercises are performed for 1–2 sets instead of the usual 3	3x15 yards	All exercises are performed for 1–2 sets instead of the usual 3
Alternating DB Incline Bench	3x8–10		3x5	
Slideboard leg curl	3x8–10 1 leg SB leg curl		3x5	
Weighted pushups	3x8–10		3x5	
Romanian dead lift (RDL)	3x8–10		3x5	

Weeks 5 & 10
Deload week of less volume usually consisting of one to two sets instead of three. Can one-rep max on bench, chinup, and hang clean on week ten.

A Few Notes

Power and core work is paired first, while the nervous system is fresh, then the strength exercises are paired in an upper body / lower body format. When the upper body is resting after a set, the lower body can be working. The brackets on the charts indicated a paired exercise. Less time standing around = more efficiency and more time to recuperate, study, etc.

All of the programs listed can add specific mobility exercises between sets to work on an individual's weak points. For example, one could do a set of TBDL then perform a set of the world's greatest stretch before moving on to chin-ups. Doing them between sets not only gives more opportunity to work on tight areas but also allows the heart rate to drop a bit before moving on to the next strength exercise. It is also a great way in large group settings to keep athletes from standing around waiting for a bench or weights to open up. More functional work done in a limited time (training density) makes for a more productive workout.

The main concern with exercise is to do no harm. If a particular lift causes joint pain, then either technique must be improved using lighter weights or an alternative exercise that doesn't cause pain must be substituted. Know the difference between muscular discomfort during lifting, which is generally okay, and pain that can cause injury if continued. Corrective exercises may be prescribed that will help the athlete eventually perform the lift without pain. Some lifts are just not suited to a particular athlete's structure or past medical history. For example, proper catching of a hang clean requires a sufficient degree of mobility in the wrists and shoulders, particularly if the athlete had a previous fracture or joint trauma. If they cause pain and corrective exercise does not solve it, then find an alternative such as a one-arm dumbbell snatch, jump squats, or clean pulls. Bench pressing is also a lift that is not for everyone. Don't be the coach or athlete who tries to put the square peg in a round hole. A great strength coach is not one who has hundreds of ways to make an exercise harder, but rather one who can regress an exercise to make it effective while pain-free.

All of the exercises listed can be found by searching them on the internet. There will be several videos for each one. My friend Dan Gabelman, current strength coach for Union College hockey and former Mike Boyle Strength and Conditioning trainer, has put together an excellent collection of short videos on YouTube under UCStrength. These videos cover numerous foam rolling, mobility, plyometrics, speed/change of direction, and strength/power exercises. All of his videos will demonstrate excellent technique as well, so as an athlete you can't go wrong with this collection as a resource.

You will see in the program samples that I have included deload weeks after four weeks of each training block. These are designed to prevent overtraining and allow the body to catch up to the intense demands it is being placed under. Theoretically, strength gains will be made this week. In a group setting, I rarely ever program them because rarely is an athlete training with 100 percent attendance for four weeks without being interrupted by school holidays, games, or other obligations. These are somewhat deload weeks themselves. Another approach instead of a deload week is to have an intro week at the beginning of each four-week bock. Week One would consist of doing two sets instead of three and learning the new movements. Week Two would add a third set, and heavier weights would be used. The intro week would serve as the deload week itself.

Chapter 13:
Effort

Perhaps the most overlooked factor in training to gain muscle and increase strength/athleticism is the amount of consistent effort that is put into it. The most sophisticated program in the world designed by the greatest of sport scientists will mean nothing if submaximal effort is used. The saying "a bad program done well is better than a great program done badly" means that poor technique and inconsistent effort will get you nowhere. I have seen several programs by some very reputable and successful teams that are less than impressive on paper. They may lack balance between pushing and pulling and hip and knee dominant movements, have very little single-leg emphasis, and be full of gimmicky exercises among other factors. Instead of being overly critical of the program design or attributing their success to the great athletes they recruit (which in reality is a huge reason for a team's success), I realize the best quality of the strength coach may be his/her ability to get the players to consistently give maximum effort in training.

I often see athletes just going through the motions with their training. They do speed development drills at ninety percent instead of a hundred percent. They do five reps as prescribed with a weight that they could've done seven or more with, if pushed. For example, sometimes I will have my athletes max out on rear elevated split squats (Bulgarian squats) by having them perform as many reps as possible with the same weight they last performed for five reps. Nearly everyone can do a significant number more. One very high level rugby girl who normally did five reps with a seventy-pound dumbbell in each hand did twenty reps when testing and encouraged. The same can be said for nutrition. Athletes say they'll drink a post-workout drink when they get home instead of having it with them at the gym ready to drink after the last set.

The human body is resilient to change. It must be forced to adapt to stressful demands that it undergoes. The SAID principle asserts that the human body adapts specifically to imposed demands. However, the human body requires these demands to be great enough to cause adaptation. This is one reason that someone new to training with weights can improve at a rapid rate the first several months. The neurological and muscular systems must adapt to this new stimulus. As one gets more experienced, the stressors must be greater to cause adaptation. The extreme end of this scale is poor programming that stresses the body too intensely and causes overtraining, sometimes in the form of injury or rhabdomyolysis, which is a breakdown of muscle tissue that releases a damaging protein into the blood. Rhabdo is a serious medical condition and is nothing to be strived for as a "badge of honor" as with some workout systems.

The key to stressing the muscles enough to cause adaptation but not to harmful levels is to use maximum effort but for only a few sets of each exercise, effort that requires the athlete to grind out the last seemingly impossible rep or two while still maintaining good form. These last few reps that require maximum effort are the ones that cause the muscles to adapt by growing larger and stronger. If safe technique is compromised during a set, then the set is ended due to technical failure. If three sets are prescribed of a particular exercise, the first set is a moderately heavy warmup, set two is a "go for it set" where a slightly heavier weight is attempted than the previous week (typically five pounds but can be even one to two pounds), and set three is based on how well set two was performed. If the desired reps weren't obtained, then decrease the weight. If the reps were reached and the athlete feels he/she could do more, then a slight increase can be made. Sometimes a third set is not even necessary if set two leaves the athlete totally spent.

Attempting to add weight each week to the lifts, even if it is only one to five pounds will keep the body adapting. The use of 1.0-pound Olympic plates or 1.25-pound magnetic plate-mates make small increases possible. The athlete won't be able to add weight forever, but you will be surprised how long you can continue to add before progress stalls. At that point other variables such as rep tempo, changing exercises, or different periodization programming can be used to create a new stimulus that causes adaptation. Sprint training and plyometrics should also be done with max efforts and not simply completed by going through the motions. As the outlaw Josey Wales, as played by Clint Eastwood, says, "Sometimes you gotta get just mad dog mean." This applies to putting maximum effort in the weight room or sprint/plyo area as well if adaptations of increased muscle, strength, and speed are to be realized.

Chapter 14:
Monitoring Strength Progress

Monitoring strength progress is essential to prevent athletes from just going through the motions in the weight room. Many will just grab a weight they think is heavy enough and use that weight week after week and month after month. The athlete's bodies will quickly adapt to this load while strength and size levels will stagnate. The following will explain a system I have evolved to in order to simplify things for those who train groups.

In my early years of training groups of athletes, primarily groups of eight to twelve aged thirteen to eighteen, I gave each athlete a sheet that they would use to record the reps and load used for each set they performed. This system worked well for those who were very organized and detailed. I could glance at their sheets and see if they were progressing from week to week. However, many would spend too much time recording and not enough time lifting. After a few years I modified this to having them record only their top weight successfully used in the three sets typically prescribed. This allowed for more time lifting and less time writing. When I started this program with a high school football team, I started noticing several sheets were filled out incorrectly, not at all, or left on the floor for me to pick up. Instead of getting mad at the players, I came up with a better solution. The players had just come from being in class all day, and the last thing they wanted to do was keep up with more numbers and record them. This is one reason I don't use percentage-based programs. Besides having very accurate and updated max lifts, I didn't want the athletes to be constantly checking a percentage board to determine their loads when they should be using their limited time to actually lift. I certainly didn't want to keep up with prescribed loads for a group of eighty fourteen- to eighteen-year-old athletes. I am a firm believer in Mike Boyle's KISS approach of simply having them try to add five pounds a week to their lifts.

The solution was to develop a dry-erase board that would be placed on the wall and be easy to access and see for each athlete. Each athlete would write his/her name in the left hand vertical column, and some of the main lifts and reps would be written on the top horizontal column. Typical exercises I recorded would be a five rep trap bar deadlift, three rep hang clean, five rep chin-up, five rep rear elevated split squat, five rep bench, and five rep incline DB press. Not all lifts were included because I believe correct technique is sacrificed with certain exercises or with lifts such as one rep TBDL. The athlete would establish a top weight used successfully for the particular exercise and then record the weight on the board. The next week when the lift was prescribed again, the athlete could look at the board and try to beat that number by five pounds or so. If he/she was able to successfully use a heavier weight or do more chin-ups etc., they would then erase the old number and write the new number in. If the lifting phase changed and the reps changed, they simply changed the exercise on the board and established a new training max to record.

This system allows the athlete to quickly glance at the board before lifting to give them a target load to shoot for. It also allows the coach to look at the board and determine if an athlete is not using enough weight for that workout or too much weight, determined by a breakdown of technique. No individual sheets means less time writing and more time lifting, and fewer unfilled charts / pencils to pick up off the floor post workout. It also allows some competitiveness amongs the athletes to try to get stronger than their teammates when they can see what they're lifting.

Although I am not a big fan of "max day" for young athletes or having a board with the ranking of the best lifters, this system promotes self-improvement each week. Also, large dry-erase boards can be expensive. I use large panels of white boards found at Home Depot and draw permanent grids with sharpies instead of marker board tape. I also use a similar system to have athletes record their daily body weight, sleep quality, what they had for breakfast, energy levels, or whatever. I want to be able to glance over during their warm-ups and make individual suggestions or modifications with training. The weight board system is not initiated until a good skill level is obtained for a beginner lifter, as I want him/her to be more concerned with correct technique instead of how much weight they can lift. Not only is this system very practical for teenage athletes, it has also been very effective for more advanced athletes as well. You can give them prescribed loads to aim for that day by looking at the board without using percentages or a computer. It might sound simple, but believe me, many have gotten extremely strong using this KISS approach.

Case Study: Ty

Ty is seventeen and went from 159 pounds to 173 in six months. He obviously wasn't carrying much body fat so the gains were muscle. He was already a workout fanatic and had a year of consistent weight training on the basic three-day program I covered in the training section. He also was a member of the High School National Championship Fitness Team and had a very high volume of pull-ups, sit-ups, push-ups, and 300-yard shuttles as part of his training at school. The extreme amount of exercise made it difficult to gain functional weight due to the high calorie demands and constantly bordering on overtraining/under-recovering. He wanted to gain some muscle after his final junior-year fitness national championship, so we made some adjustments in his program. We switched to the four-day program since his volume of training for the competitions had reduced and he had less risk of overtraining. We also went through the four- to five-week phases of higher reps followed by four to five weeks of strength training in the three to five rep zone paired with a slow eccentric-emphasized isolation exercise to increase the time under tension. He started consuming a pre-workout drink that consisted of a half serving of weight-gain powder in water (twenty grams protein/forty grams carbs). After the workout he immediately consumed a post-workout drink of the same, except in a pint of chocolate milk. He also increased his calorie intake, consisting of fifty percent carbs, thirty percent protein, and twenty percent fat. We also added more emphasis on recovery with regular ice baths (seven to ten minutes in fifty-five-degree water), soft tissue work with foam rolling and lacrosse balls, and sequential compression boots for twenty to thirty minutes of a high setting with the feet elevated. After gaining his weight while also training for function, Ty improved his laser timed ten-yard sprints and vertical jump as well, and finished third in the nation individually at the High School Fitness National Championship.

Chapter 15:
In-Season Weight Retention

The prevention of weight loss during a competitive season is crucial to both short-term and long-term success. Many sports do a poor job of emphasizing the importance of strength training and nutrition once in season. I have observed many high school football players (often the athletes most likely to desire weight gaining) spend all spring and summer getting bigger and stronger in the weight room only to stop lifting in favor of more practice time. They will lose valuable muscle during the season, as well as strength and speed. A loss of strength will most likely result in a loss of power in the form of slower speed, lower vertical jump, and more susceptibility to injury. I have commonly witnessed high school skill position players lose twenty pounds over a season because their coaches don't have them lift much at all once practice starts in August. What good does it do to be big, strong, and fast in August and lose it all by the time playoffs start in November?

Perhaps the biggest negative effect of this flawed strategy is in long-term athletic development. The off-season is the best time to make gains in muscle, strength, and speed. There are limited practices and games, and thus more time to train and recover.

When an athlete fails to at least maintain or minimize the loss of his/her strength and muscle during the season, then the first few months of off-season are spent trying to regain lost physical qualities instead of building on existing ones. The 190-pound linebacker at the beginning of August is now 172 at the beginning of off-season in December, and it takes him until mid-February to get back to 190 and return to the equivalent strength/speed. Had he trained correctly during the season, he would still be around 190 at the start of December off-season and be 205 or so while setting personal bests in the weight room in mid-February.

The inconsistent in-season training leads to an up-down-up-down progress over a three- to four-year period instead of a stair-step consistent upward progress. Long-term athletic development should be the goal of every athlete and coach. The seniors should be much more athletically and physically developed than they were as sophomores. A group of seniors properly developed over three to four years has a much greater chance of being winners instead of just being participants. These players also have a greater chance of earning college scholarships that could change their lives for the next forty years.

So the next question is how to train in season. With many hours devoted to long practices, a full program is not only not possible due to time constraints, it could lead to overtraining/under-recovery. Fortunately, a well-designed program to at least maintain and, even better, make progress in season does not have to take that much time. Two or three days a week for twenty minutes or so is 100 percent better than training once every two weeks or no lifting at all. The same basic weight program I presented in the three-day example could be used, except the athlete should keep the sets to two instead of three and the reps for the compound lifts to three to five. Combination lifts such as a hang clean + front squat or a DB RDL + curl + overhead press can also be utilized when under time constraints. At the very least, one set to failure of the lifts is certainly better than none at all and can be surprisingly effective if maximum effort is used. The high intensity/low volume approach will allow for a much better recovery while maintaining and possibly even gaining strength/size over the season. Maintaining should not ever be the goal in my opinion. Striving to make improvements, even if the results are small, insures that maximum effort is being exerted. If you're an in-season athlete, don't wait for your coaches to make time for the team to lift, because many won't. Find the time on your own, before school, after practice, or on weekends. There are 168 hours in a week. Be responsible and find the time to fit in twenty- to thirty-minute workouts two to three times a week. In the words of Coach Dan Hawkins, "This ain't intramurals, brother!"

Nutrition will be equally important with in-season training. Treat each sport practice like a weight workout and use the same pre-/post-workout feeding and supplementation strategies. The athlete will be burning lots of glycogen and tearing down muscle tissue during practice and games just as he/she would be in the weight room. Athletes should weigh themselves at the same time on the same scale each week and monitor it accordingly. If they find themselves losing more than five pounds, they should increase the calories. In hot, humid environments the athletes should be weighed before each practice to see if they are properly rehydrated from the previous day of practice. Keeping hard-earned muscle on during a season helps keep the horsepower up and performance to a maximum. In-season injuries will be reduced but not totally eliminated. When the whole team is on board with this approach, there's a much greater chance of success over the many teams that don't emphasize in-season training, especially late season when it matters the most.

Chapter 16:
Steroids

A popular topic when it comes to athletes and muscle gain/performance enhancement is steroids. Not all steroids build muscle, however. Corticosteroids are used to treat conditions such as asthma, skin rashes, and inflamed joints. Some actually weaken tendons while masking pain, and increase the odds of tendon rupture. Anabolic steroids are the ones most commonly associated with performance enhancement. They facilitate recovery and enhance strength and muscle gain as well as prevent muscle loss when on a calorie restricted diet. They are also used medically to help prevent muscle loss in AIDS or burn patients.

A lot of misinformation regarding anabolic steroids has been presented by the media, folklore, and even Congress. Many paint a picture of steroids being as lethal as any drug there is and causing millions of deaths by those who have used them. If this were the case, then hundreds of former major league baseball and football players now in their fifties and sixties would be dying at an alarming rate. Like any drug, abuse has occurred and many bodybuilders/athletes who took massive amounts in the past have had some serious medical conditions as a result. Add high levels of steroids to a personality that also uses cocaine, alcohol, meth, and other dangerous substances, and disaster is likely to occur down the road if not sooner. Some bodybuilding deaths have occurred from mismanagement of diuretics prior to a contest.

The media sometimes paint a picture of widespread use among teenage athletes. I personally find this to be untrue. I have trained hundreds of young athletes over the past twenty years and have only heard the word steroids mentioned in a conversation maybe once or twice. Steroids are not as easily accessible as they were in the 1980s and are costly to get. They may be fake and ineffective, too. Drug testing makes it not worth the risk. I'm not saying that some high school and college athletes aren't taking steroids, but I think the numbers are very small compared to the numbers who don't. The abuse of alcohol and prescription pain meds is a problem with teens that the media and Congress don't seem to be as concerned about as they are about the moral dilemma of cheating in sports. Kids are *much* more concerned about getting booze, hydrocodone, and weed than they are steroids.

Some think that steroids are magic. They don't work that way. If they did, there would be thousands walking around like "those guys on the magazine covers." You still have to train hard and you still have to eat a lot for them to be effective. Sport science has made such tremendous strides that they aren't needed for a young athlete to put on muscle. Football players today are bigger, faster, and stronger naturally than those in the "steroid era" of the 1980s. The plans outlined in this book have been proven over time to work. Paying attention to recovery, nutrition, and smart programming/consistency can lead to far better gains than for those who don't follow that regimen but take steroids. Some will think about using steroids while not even trying to get one+ gram of protein per body weight first, sufficiently stay hydrated, or just randomly lift.

A major reason why young athletes shouldn't take steroids is that their bodies are already producing a tremendous cocktail of anabolic hormones naturally. For the young athlete testosterone and growth hormones are at an all-time high, and any use of anabolic steroids while this hormone avalanche is occurring only risks suppressing the body's natural production. There is a huge risk of the body saying that it already is getting too much from the drug and it doesn't need to be producing more. Sometimes this can be reversed once off the steroids, and sometimes it can remain suppressed for a lifetime. A doctor who is an expert on the subject has told me stories of young men who have permanently suppressed their natural production from using only one injection of a particular testosterone blend. Don't risk it, either, with taking the "natural" precursors of testosterone boosting supplements. If you think you aren't producing enough testosterone naturally, then get blood work done. There are some cases of this occurring even with twenty-year-old males with no history of steroid use. On a side note, regular alcohol consumption can have a huge negative effect on testosterone production. If you are truly concerned about maximizing your hormone production, then stop drinking!

I feel that most reading this book will be athletes trying to gain muscle/strength to enhance their sport performance instead of bodybuilders simply trying to gain muscle for looks or competitions. I at least wanted to touch on the subject and advise maximizing your potential through smart training, consistent effort, and great nutritional planning. Plus, nobody has gotten busted for these attributes like some have from dealing with steroids. In an age of frequent drug testing, don't risk being suspended from a game, being expelled from a team and losing a scholarship, or being labeled a cheater the rest of your career.

Chapter 17:
The Best We Can Be

I hope this book has helped you or a trainee of yours in your quest to gain weight. It is often not as complicated as it seems but it does take a dedicated effort to consistently train and feed. Doing the same thing with no results while hoping things magically happen is not only non productive, it is also stupid. Many still choose to do this and end up frustrated as a result. As an athlete, you want your weight gained to be functional and to make you more athletic. This system of training and eating that I've shared with you has been proven to work with many athletes who have gone on to have great success—many have even earned college scholarships worth $100,000 or more. Some may gain faster than others due to genetics, but we can all improve and strive to be the best version of ourselves that we can possibly be.

About the Author

Sean Ross has been a Certified Strength and Conditioning Specialist since 1994. He is a graduate of Christian Brothers High School in Memphis, Tennessee, and he earned a degree in Occupational Therapy from the University of Central Arkansas. After working as an Occupational Therapist for many years, he opened Ross Strength and Speed in Little Rock, Arkansas, in 2004. He has trained athletes from a number of different sports at all different levels to enhance their athletic ability. He is also certified by USA Weightlifting, Precision Nutrition, and has completed several mentorships with Mike Boyle Strength and Conditioning and EXOS.

www.ingramcontent.com/pod-product-compliance
Lightning Source LLC
Chambersburg PA
CBHW071331190426
43193CB00041B/1567